The Legend of Arthur in British and American Literature

Twayne's English Authors Series

Kinley Roby, Editor

Northeastern University

TEAS 461

THE LADY OF THE LAKE
TELLETH ARTHVR OF THE
SWORD EXCALIBVR

ILLUSTRATION BY AUBREY BEARDSLEY FOR SIR THOMAS MALORY'S
MORTE D'ARTHUR. LONDON 1893–94.
By permission of the Houghton Library, Harvard University

The Legend of Arthur in British and American Literature

By Jennifer R. Goodman

Texas A. & M. University

Twayne Publishers

A Division of G.K. Hall & Co. • Boston

The Legend of Arthur in British and American Literature

Jennifer R. Goodman

Copyright 1988 by G.K. Hall & Co.
All rights reserved.
Published by Twayne Publishers
A Division of G.K. Hall & Co.
70 Lincoln Street
Boston, Massachusetts 02111

Copyediting supervised by Barbara Sutton
Book production by Gabrielle B. McDonald
Book design by Barbara Anderson

Typeset in 11 pt. Garamond
by Williams Press, Inc., Albany, New York

Printed on permanent/durable acid-free paper
and bound in the United States of America

Library of Congress Cataloging-in-Publication Data

Goodman, Jennifer R. (Jennifer Robin), 1953-
   The legend of Arthur in British and American literature.

   (Twayne's English authors series; TEAS 461)
   Bibliography: p. 138
   Includes index.
   1. Arthurian romances—History and criticism.
2. English literature—History and criticism.
3. American literature—History and criticism.
I. Title.   II. Series.
PR149.A79G66   1988   820'.9'351   87–28144
ISBN 0–8057–6965–X (alk. paper)

To the memory of Laila Zamuelis Gross

Contents

About the Author

Jennifer R. Goodman, assistant professor of English at Texas A. & M. University, received her Bachelor of Arts degree in medieval history and literature from Radcliffe College, and holds Master of Arts degrees in medieval studies from the University of Toronto and in English from Harvard University, as well as a Doctorate of Philosophy in English from Harvard. She is a member of Phi Beta Kappa, the Modern Language Association of America, the Medieval Academy of America, the New Chaucer Society, the International Arthurian Society, the International Courtly Literature Society, and the Southeastern Medieval Association.

Professor Goodman has published articles on Malory and Caxton, Chaucer, Captain John Smith, and theater history. Her work has appeared in *Studies in the Age of Chaucer, Virginia Magazine of History and Biography,* and the *Harvard Library Bulletin.* In *The Legend of Arthur in British and American Literature* she explores the origins and continuing strength of the primary epic tradition in the English-speaking world.

Preface

Since his first appearance in the fifth century A.D., King Arthur has inspired a long series of infinitely various legends and literary works. No other subject has evoked a wider range of writings. The story of Arthur has been recognized since the seventeenth century, if not earlier, as the chief epic subject for English-speaking writers. He has been depicted as a messianic figure, a utopian visionary, an ideal leader. He has been employed in bedroom farce and in political satire. His court, similarly, has been seen as representing everything from perfected human society to a seething mass of uncontrollable passions.

In many ways, the history of the Arthurian legends in English and American literature is also a history of that literature in general. Over fifteen centuries diverse intellectual movements have reshaped the story of Arthur and the Round Table to suit their own purposes. Transitions among them are often revealed more clearly in Arthurian literature than elsewhere. Because the plot remains more or less familiar, readers of Arthurian works can focus on the altered treatment of the story. Changes in Arthurian literature mirror changes in our knowledge and beliefs about ourselves and our history. Theories of the rise and fall of civilization, the expansion of popular literature, and the influence of new trends in scholarship all find their reflections in Arthurian literature.

This compact volume examines the history of the Arthurian legends and their role in English and American literature up to the present. It presents a connected overview of the subject, offering its readers the chance to scan the realm of Arthurian literature in brief compass. Like an aerial photograph, it necessarily focuses on long perspectives rather than providing close-range studies of any one work or author. For both general readers and students of Arthurian literature, this volume should serve as an introductory foray into a massive subject, certainly not as the last word on it. References to editions and works of modern Arthurian scholarship allow interested readers to pursue specific topics in greater depth. I have also suggested translations and useful general works where appropriate.

At the same time, this is necessarily a personal history of Arthur, grounded as much as possible on fresh readings of major primary sources. The Arthurian specialist who reads these pages will recognize a number of idiosyncratic conclusions: I have attempted to indicate clearly where my own thinking diverges from the main stream of Arthurian studies. My own research in later medieval chivalric romance and in stage history leads me to different approaches in many cases than those of earlier scholars, and perhaps to an altered view of the entire subject. While it is centered in English and American literature, this account also remarks on the continuing vitality and importance of the European tradition of Arthurian literature. Emphasis is laid on key cross influences from non-Arthurian legends, history, and literature that have altered the portrayal of Arthur and his world. Some necessary attention is also paid here to social and historical contexts of Arthurian literature, and to neglected genres, although Arthurian narrative poetry and prose remain at the center of the discussion.

For their help in the preparation of this book I am grateful, first to those past and present scholars whose primary Arthurian researches make such efforts at synthesis possible. My analysis necessarily rests on the work of Roger Sherman Loomis and Laura Hibbard Loomis, Eugène Vinaver, Geoffrey Ashe, Richard Barber, Elisabeth Brewer and Beverley Taylor, Norris J. Lacy, Raymond Thompson, James Wilhelm, and the many distinguished contributors to R. S. Loomis's *Arthurian Literature in the Middle Ages: A Collaborative History* (London: Oxford University Press, 1959) and the *Arthurian Encyclopedia* (New York: Garland, 1986). Their studies remain fundamental to all Arthurian scholarship.

The frontispiece of this volume is reproduced by permission of the Houghton Library, Harvard University. I am grateful to the staff of the Houghton Library, in particular to Dr. Jeanne T. Newlin and Martha Mahard of the Harvard Theater Collection, for their resourcefulness and friendship. I would also like to thank the staffs of Firestone Library at Princeton University and the O. Meredith Wilson Library at the University of Minnesota for their hospitality during the summers of 1985 and 1986.

Jennifer R. Goodman

Texas A. & M. University

Chronology

This chronology lists important historical events and works concerned with Arthur. Dates in brackets are approximate; they are based on the most recent editorial or historical consensus on each item.

43	Beginning of the Roman conquest of Britain.
383–410	Gradual withdrawal of Roman troops from Britain.
468–469 or 470	Campaign of British king "Riothamus" in Gaul, identified by Geoffrey Ashe as a prototype of Arthur.
[500]	Approximate date of the battle of Mount Badon, traditionally associated with the historical Arthur.
539	Date of the battle of Camlann, where "Arthur and Medraut fell," according to the *Annales Cambriae*.
[547]	Gildas, *De excidio et conquestu Britanniae (On the Destruction and Conquest of Britain)*.
[sixth century]	Taliesin, *Elegy for Owain Son of Urien*.
[600–]	Aneirin, *The Gododdin*. First mentions Arthur's name.
731	Bede, *Ecclesiastical History of the English Nation*.
[800]	Nennius, *Historia Brittonum (History of the Britons)*.
[ninth to tenth century]	"The Stanzas of the Graves" in *The Black Book of Carmarthen*.
[900–]	*Annales Cambriae (The Annals of Cambria)*.
[tenth to eleventh century]	"Geraint filius Erbin" in *The Black Book of Carmarthen*.
1019	*The Legend of Saint Goeznovius*.
[1100]	*Culhwch and Olwen*.
[1125]	William of Malmesbury, *Gesta regum Anglorum (Deeds of the Kings of the English)*.
[1136–1138]	Geoffrey of Monmouth, *Historia regum Britanniae (History of the Kings of Britain)*.

1155	Wace, *Roman de Brut.*
fl. 1155–1190	Chrétien de Troyes: *Erec et Enide, Cligès, Lancelot, Yvain, Perceval.*
[1195–]	Giraldus Cambrensis, *De instructione principis (On the Education of Princes).*
[1200–1230]	French Vulgate Cycle prose romances.
[1205]	Layamon, *Brut.*
[1350–1400]	Alliterative *Morte Arthure.*
[ca. 1370]	*Sir Gawain and the Green Knight.*
[1393–1394]	Geoffrey Chaucer, "The Wife of Bath's Tale."
[1375–1400]	Stanzaic *Morte Arthur.*
1469	Sir Thomas Malory, *Morte Darthur* completed.
1485	William Caxton publishes Malory's *Morte Darthur.*
1512–1513	Polydore Vergil's *Anglica Historia* dismisses Arthur.
1544	John Leland, *Assertio inclytissimi Arturii.*
1587	Thomas Hughes and others, *The Misfortunes of Arthur.*
[1590–1596]	Edmund Spenser, *The Faerie Queene.*
1609	Ben Johnson, *The Speeches at Prince Henry's Barriers.*
1662	William Rowley, *The Birth of Merlin.*
1691	John Dryden, *King Arthur: The British Worthy,* opera with music by Henry Purcell.
1695	Sir Richard Blackmore, *Prince Arthur.*
1813	Sir Walter Scott, "The Bridal of Triermain."
1829	Thomas Love Peacock, *The Misfortunes of Elphin.*
1842	Alfred, Lord Tennyson, "Morte d'Arthur."
1849	Edward Bulwer-Lytton, *King Arthur.*
1852	Matthew Arnold, "Tristram and Iseult."
1858	William Morris, *The Defence of Guenevere and Other Poems.*
1859–1872	Alfred, Lord Tennyson, *Idylls of the King.*
1865	Richard Wagner, *Tristan und Isolde.*

1882   Algernon Swinburne, *Tristram of Lyonnesse.*

1889   Mark Twain, *A Connecticut Yankee in King Arthur's Court.*

1895   J. Comyns Carr, *King Arthur: A Drama.*

1922   T. S. Eliot, *The Waste Land.*

1923   Thomas Hardy, *The Famous Tragedy of the Queen of Cornwall at Tintagel in Lyonnesse.*

1927   Edwin Arlington Robinson, *Tristram.*

1932   John Cowper Powys, *A Glastonbury Romance.*

1938   Charles Williams, *Taliesin through Logres.*

1958   T. H. White, *The Once and Future King.*

1960   Alan J. Lerner and Frederick Loewe, *Camelot.*

1970–1979   Mary Stewart, *The Crystal Cave; The Hollow Hills; The Last Enchantment.*

1975   *Monty Python and the Holy Grail* (film).

1976   John Steinbeck, *The Acts of King Arthur.*

1980   Parke Godwin, *Firelord.*

1981   *Excalibur* (film, directed by John Boorman).

1982   Marion Zimmer Bradley, *The Mists of Avalon.*

1983   Mary Stewart, *The Wicked Day.*

Chapter One

The Origins of Arthur: From History to Legend

King Arthur has been enthroned as a reigning hero of our civilization for a long time. The urge to retell his story seems to be perennial to the Western imagination. If the volume of existing Arthurian literature was unbelievable in the fifteenth century, when William Caxton called it "a world / or a thyng incredyble to byleue," it is even more extraordinary today.

On first looking into this venerable and extensive body of lore, readers almost invariably ask if an Arthur ever really lived. The question is important, though it is not one that can be answered to our complete satisfaction. It does not simply reflect a prejudice against fiction and in favor of true stories, or society's need to connect itself with a heroic past. Rather, the issue of Arthur's real existence seems to spring from the idealistic character of the Arthurian legend itself. King Arthur has more to prove to his readers than other heroes because Arthurian works often provide more than basic entertainment. As the literature developed, Arthur quickly became an ideal ruler, and his court an idealized society that made explicit demands for moral, religious, and social responsibility upon its members, and by extension upon its readers. Reading such an Arthurian work can become an act of faith, of commitment. Caxton told the readers of Malory's *Morte Darthur* "for to gyve fayth and byleve that al is trewe that is conteyned herin ye be at your lyberté," but historically many readers have always wished to believe, and indeed to accept Arthur's vision as a worthy model for their own lives. A living role model is inevitably more reassuring than a purely fictional one.

This initial chapter traces the forging of the legend from historical materials. It travels from fragmentary fifth and sixty-century historical and archaeological evidence to the explosion of Arthurian literature in the twelfth century. Returning to Arthur's point of origin, it observes the legend beginning to coalesce around its historical core. Even the fragmentary and tantalizing evidence at our disposal permits some conclusions about the actual events at the center of Arthurian mythology.

The Historical Setting

To locate King Arthur historically, investigators must trace him back beyond chivalry, feudalism, and knighthood to the late antique period, and the collapse of Roman Britain. Arthur is in fact older than "England" or the English, and certainly much older than the English language that celebrates him. More than one commentator has enjoyed the paradox that England's most famous national hero seems to have achieved his fame in combat against the ancestors of the English.

For information on Arthur's origins, the student of English and American literature turns to experts with complementary perspectives on early Britain: Roman and Anglo-Saxon historians, Celtic scholars, medieval Latinists, and archaeologists. These specialists agree in placing any historical Arthur in approximately the fifth or the early sixth century, at the time when the old Roman province of Britannia was experiencing Germanic migrations from the Frisian lands and the Danish peninsula, the beginnings of the Anglo-Saxon invasions. Each field of specialization helps to picture the historical circumstances that gave rise to the legend of Arthur.

Historians of Roman Britain like S.S. Frere and Peter Salway remind us that fifth-century Britannia had been a Roman province for four hundred years, one sufficiently important to the empire, and sufficiently troublesome, to justify the deployment of one tenth of the Roman army to keep it in order.[1] At its most prosperous, Roman Britain boasted impressive country estates. The spectacular villa excavated at Fishbourne in Sussex is perhaps the best known today, though less opulent complexes like the one at Ditchley in Oxfordshire seem more typical. Archaeologists continue to investigate towns like Bath, to mention only the most famous, with its thermal center, temples, and public buildings, and major military camps and fortifications like Hadrian's wall, as well as the Romans' effective road and signaling systems, and their factories for the production of pottery and woolen goods.[2]

Celtic tribal organization coexisted to some degree in the south with Roman civil and military administrative structures, though the Picts in northwestern Scotland and the Irish to the west remained threats to the province. On the religious front, official Roman cults were practiced alongside the worship of a variety of Celtic nature gods and goddesses, and Eastern mystery religions like Mithraism.[3] By the late fourth century Britain had an established Christian community that sent its bishops to councils in Gaul and produced the eloquent Pelagius and his influential heresy.[4] The visit of Saint Germanus in 429 to combat the spread of Pelagianism among the British Christians required him to outface a sizable community of wayward believers. Salway emphasizes contacts and parallels between the experience of Roman rule in Gaul and in Britain; Geoffrey Ashe also stresses these links as important to the proper understanding of fifth-century history.[5]

By the second half of the fourth century, imperial claims by British commanders and troubles elsewhere in the empire were leading to the gradual disappearance of most Roman troops from their British bases. Rather than a sudden retreat, the Roman army's departure from Britain was gradual, carried out over approximately a thirty-year period. The military commander Magnus Maximus brought a substantial force from Britain to Gaul in 383 to assert his claim to imperial position. The general Stilicho transferred more troops to Italy in 401–2 to protect Rome against its own barbarian invaders. Constantine III followed Maximus's example in withdrawing his own contingent to the Continent in 407, again to support his pretensions to the title of emperor. The Greek historian Zosimus indicates that some remnants of the Roman army remained in Britain as late as 409, but the famous letter he reports from the emperor Honorius, directing cities to undertake their own defense, does not find these last outposts of empire worth mentioning.[6]

The early fifth century in Britain seems to have been marked by a serious breakdown in central administration. The void was evidently filled to some degree by local magnates. The best known of these figures is the man the ninth-century monk Nennius calls "Vortigern," a title rather than a personal name, perhaps meaning "supreme ruler." In later Arthurian literature, Vortigern becomes infamous for his ill-advised importation of Saxon mercenaries to settle in Britain. Historians and archaeologists disagree over the extent to which Romanized life survived in Britain as that province became increasingly more isolated from the beleaguered empire. Some evidence suggests that a number of walled towns and villas continued to be occupied, especially in the southwest, even as Roman Britain was coming under pressure from the Saxons. Leslie Alcock's excavations at South Cadbury in Devonshire suggest the hill-fort there was a major military base in the fourth century. At the same time, the British appear in Brittany and elsewhere in Gaul, beginning a countermigration that was to make this Celtic-speaking race the dominant force on that peninsula.[7]

The idea of massive "Anglo-Saxon invasions" overwhelming Roman Britain in the fifth and sixth centuries has gone out of fashion in recent years. The latest archaeological evidence tends to lower estimates of the size of the Anglo-Saxon migration, and suggest that provincial society was already deteriorating from within during the fourth century.[8] This revised view pictures a gradual transition from Roman to Anglo-Saxon civilization, punctuated by local hostilities, rather than the period of widespread violence graphically described in the inflammatory writings of the sixty-century moralist Gildas. The student of the Arthurian legend must reconsider Arthur's historical origins in the light of this new reconstruction of fifth-century life.

Gildas and the displaced Britons of Brittany may indeed have embellished both the legend of Arthur and legendary Anglo-Saxon invasions in order to explain their historical circumstances in heroic terms. Clearly, though, if Arthur never existed, it was imperative to invent him.

Early Latin Sources

From this general picture of the historical circumstances leading to the rise of the Arthurian legend, attention must now shift to the earliest written sources that depict fifth- and sixth-century Britain. Many of the earliest surviving records concerning this period are difficult or proble-matical to interpret. Scholarship must often diverge into speculation or conjecture as it analyzes them.[9] This section discusses both the nature of the sources and the problems they pose their interpreters.

Gildas, *De excidio et conquestu Britanniae (On the Destruction and Conquest of Britain).* The first important Latin source for the late fifth and early sixth century is Gildas's polemical treatise, *De excidio et conquestu Britanniae (On the Destruction and Conquest of Britain).*[10] Little information is available about Gildas's life. He was apparently a monk writing in the west of England, possibly in Chester, around 540. His treatise surveys British history up to his own day in order to denounce his contemporaries for failing to live up to the standards of the past under the continuing stresses of Saxon expansion. This attitude may well have warped Gildas's view of history. It also links Gildas to a favorite theme of future Arthurian literature, the contrast between a heroic former age and the degenerate present.

Gildas's account of fifth- and sixth-century Britain in his twenty-third chapter describes the arrival of "Saxon" mercenaries, invited by a "proud tyrant" that modern scholars identify with the British magnate called Vortigern by later sources. Such an invitation to a barbarian people would hardly have been an original notion on Vortigern's part. It recalls the Roman policy of enlisting barbarian warriors—"federate troops"—to assist the regular imperial forces.[11] According to Gildas, these Saxons intended to protect the Romanized Britons against their local enemies, the marauding Picts and Scots to the north and Irish raiders to the west. In Gildas's account the venture turned out badly, as the Saxons soon proved more dangerous than the Britons' original foes. Gildas, writing not as an objective modern historian, but as a moralist castigating his contemporaries, offers graphic descriptions of the precarious survival and miseries of the fugitive Britons.[12]

This is the historical setting in which Arthur's legend has most often been placed. Yet Gildas, the source closest to the critical period, never mentions an Arthur, or an Artorius, as the name would appear in Latin.[13] He does identify one Ambrosius Aurelianus as the British leader who first rallied his people against the Saxons.[14] Was Ambrosius Aurelianus the original Arthur? Was he some relative, as William of Malmesbury stated early in the twelfth century? It is impossible to tell from Gildas's text. Gildas is much more anxious to express his disgust at the failures of Ambrosius's sixth-century descendants than he is to offer corroborative historical details.

Gildas also mentions the siege of Mount Badon as the great British victory of the era, a battle whose physical location has so far eluded modern scholars. A site in southwestern England, near Bath or Swindon, is currently in favor.[15] Gildas describes this conflict as "the last but certainly not the least" defeat of the Anglo-Saxon forces. Maddeningly, Gildas neglects to insert the name of any victorious British commander. But this battle was later identified as Arthur's major triumph.

Gildas's vague dating has also puzzled readers. The Venerable Bede understood Gildas to mean that the battle of Mount Badon occurred in 493, not an impossible date, but other interpretations are possible.[16] Gildas, then, must be regarded as an elusive, excitable, and highly selective source. He unquestionably sets the stage for the rise of the Arthurian legend, but his text does not initiate it.

The Venerable Bede, *Historia Ecclesiastica Gentis Anglorum (Ecclesiastical History of the English Nation).* The next Latin source to take up the early history of Britain, the Venerable Bede's

Ecclesiastical History of the English Nation of around 731, is vastly
more reliable. Bede (673?–735) has been ranked as the greatest scholar
Anglo-Saxon England produced. His *Ecclesiastical History* remains one
of the most impressive historical works of the Middle Ages. Unfortunately, Bede adds little to Gildas, beyond his reasonable attempt to
sort out the chronology of Mount Badon. Parallels in the wording of
the two works make it clear that Bede used Gildas as a direct source.
He also mentions Ambrosius Aurelianus. He does not name Arthur.[17]

Nennius, *Historia Brittonum* (*History of the Britons*). For the
first appearance of someone called "Arthur" in any Latin historical
work, one must turn to the *Historia Brittonum* (*History of the Britons*)
written around 800 by an author traditionally identified as a Welshman
called Nennius.[18] Nennius asserts that Arthur led "the kings of Britain"
against the Saxons as "their leader of battles." He lists twelve en-
gagements between Arthur's forces and the Saxons, the last of the twelve
being the celebrated battle of Mount Badon, "in which nine hundred
and sixty men fell from a single attack of Arthur." It has proven
difficult to substantiate Nennius's geographical references, and both the
numbers twelve and 960 may betray a standard medieval regard for
numbers as being symbolic rather than factual. Nennius locates one
battle in the Caledonian forest of Scotland. Another at the "city of the
Legion" may refer to Caerleon in Wales. Frere points out that seven
of the twelve battles are associated with rivers. He suggests that this
feature reflects a strategy of aiming attacks at river crossings, where a
small cavalry force could gain an advantage over more numerous bodies
of warriors on foot.[19] Generally Nennius's place-names take Arthur
farther north than most modern historical conjectures would place him,
though some respected scholars have written persuasively in favor of an
Arthur based in northern Britain.[20]

Three further points drawn from literary analysis of Nennius deserve
mention here. First, Nennius refers to Arthur not as a king, but as a
war leader directing the activities of local British rulers. Second, Nennius's
Arthur is unmistakably a Christian champion routing pagan enemies.[21]
A third factor to consider is the clear evidence Nennius presents for
the accretion of Welsh legendary material around the story of Arthur.
Aside from his main narrative in chapter 56, Nennius also refers to
Arthur in chapter 73, where he describes two places associated with
Arthur. He first relates the miraculous preservation of a footprint of
Arthur's dog Cabal in a rock on a certain cairn, and then describes
the marvelous tomb of Arthur's son Anir, which can never be measured.

These two references begin a long history of place-name legends that link Arthur to specific locations. Nennius is evidently aware of some traditions concerning a great boar hunt in which Arthur took part.[22] A boar hunt is also a central event in the flamboyant Arthurian tale of *Culhwch and Olwen* (see Section Three). On the occasion of his name's first appearance in a historical work, Arthur is already a figure enveloped in legend.

The Annals of Cambria (Annales Cambriae). Arthur's career is also documented in *The Annals of Cambria (Annales Cambriae),* probably written in the 900s. Three Arthurian entries give late but possible dates for the battle of Mount Badon (516), for the battle of Camlann (537) "in which Arthur and Medraut fell" and for Gildas's death (570).[23] This first recorded mention of Camlann and Medraut is tantalizingly ambiguous, as the twentieth-century novelist Mary Stewart points out in support of her own fictional rehabilitation of Mordred (see Chapter 5). Were Medraut-Mordred and Arthur fighting on the same side or against one another? Where was Camlann located? Again, the text yields no further data.

The Legend of Saint Goeznovius. The next item of Latin evidence is the anonymous Latin *Legend of Saint Goeznovius,* a life of the sixth- or seventh-century Saint Goueznou of Brittany. This work bore the date 1019; it survives today only as excerpts in a fifteenth-century manuscript of the *Chronicle of Saint Brieuc.* As Geoffrey Ashe observed in his 1981 *Speculum* article, *Goeznovius's* introduction describes Vortigern's admission of the Saxons to Britain, and reports that this first Saxon outbreak was halted by "the great Arthur, King of the Britons," who succeeded in driving the Saxons for the most part out of Britain. "But when this same Arthur, after many victories which he won gloriously in Britain and Gaul, was summoned at last from human activity, the way was open for the Saxons."[24] Ashe regards this testimony as particularly important, first, because it apparently corroborates Geoffrey of Monmouth's twelfth-century report of Arthur's campaigns in France. Second, Ashe directs scholarly attention to the neglected figure of "Riothamus," a word that is, like "Vortigern," a title rather than a personal name. Ashe's "Riothamus" seems to have been a British leader of around 440–70 whose campaign against the Visigoths culminated in the treachery of his Gallo-Roman allies and in defeat near Bourg-de-Déols in France. This Riothamus is mentioned in Jordanes's *History of the Goths,* and addressed in a letter by that energetic correspondent Sidonius Apollinaris, bishop of Clermont-Ferrand. Ashe observes that

Riothamus's dates suit both Geoffrey of Monmouth's placement of Arthur in the reign of Emperor Leo I at Constantinople (457–74) and Leslie Alcock's evidence for the massive refortification of the hilltop at South Cadbury, a possible prototype for Camelot. He suggests that Riothamus's disappearance from history, perhaps near Avallon in France, might also connect with the later tradition of the mortally wounded Arthur's departure for the isle of Avalon. Ashe's article concludes by proposing either that Riothamus's Continental exploits contributed to a later composite figure of Arthur, or that an "Artorius Riothamus" was in fact the true Arthur of history. Later battles associated with Arthur-Riothamus would then be the work of his men, still fighting as a unit, or would have been attributed to Arthur as his legend gathered materials not originally related to it.

Ashe's advocacy of Riothamus certainly offers an alternative to existing Arthurian speculations. It demonstrates that Arthur's exact historical location has by no means been settled, any more than the question of whether there was even a single Arthur. Ashe's work complicates the picture of the end of Roman Britain, but also clarifies it. The same Arthurian scholars who deplore the notion of an entirely new candidate for the title of "the historical Arthur" must rejoice in Ashe's citation of primary materials going beyond the familiar English and Welsh sources for this period. Ashe may make it more difficult to identify an Arthur, but he also makes it clear that there may be history as well as legend in later accounts of Arthur's Continental activities. On the balance, Arthur emerges from Ashe's article a more plausibly "historical" figure than he began.

William of Malmesbury and Gerald of Wales.   Two twelfth-century comments on Arthur complete this discussion of his documentation in the Latin histories. The Benedictine monk William of Malmesbury (ca. 1095–1143), one of the best-regarded historians of his own day, associates Arthur with Ambrosius in his account of the British-Saxon conflicts in his *Gesta Regum Anglorum (Deeds of the Kings of the English)* of around 1125. William seems to recall Gildas and Bede in his accounts of Vortigern and Ambrosius, and Nennius in his description of Arthur's slaughter of nine hundred Saxons at Mount Badon. He diverges from these predecessors interestingly by connecting Arthur and Ambrosius, and by signaling the existence of a body of unspecified Breton Arthurian legends. "This is the Arthur about whom the trifles of the Bretons rave even now, one certainly not to be dreamed of in false myths, but proclaimed in truthful histories."[25] William of Malmesbury also mentions "Walwen," later Gawain, as Arthur's nephew, and passes along varying traditions of his death, either wounded and shipwrecked, or betrayed at a feast. Both versions find echoes in later accounts of Gawain. This discussion of Walwen and his tomb allows the twelfth-century historian to note the contrast between Gawain's rediscovered sepulchre and the unknown tomb of Arthur, from which the great king may one day return.

A tomb of Arthur was indeed rediscovered before the end of the twelfth century. This signal event in the early history of Arthurian archaeology is chronicled by Gerald de Barri (ca. 1146–1223), also known by his Latinized name of Giraldus Cambrensis (Gerald of Wales), in his *On the Education of Princes (De instructione principis)* of around 1195.[26] Giraldus's narrative points out that rumors of Arthur's survival and potential return to reunite the Celtic peoples and lead them to victory had been greatly exaggerated. Arthur's tomb had already been excavated at Glastonbury Abbey. Giraldus further informs his readers that he himself has seen the marble tomb to which the monks had removed the bones they had unearthed, and had verified the inscription on the cross discovered with the remains: "Here lies buried the famous King Arthur with Guinevere [Wenneveria] his second wife on the Island of Avalon."[27] This cross with its inscription was reproduced in William Camden's *Britannia* of 1607, though the cross itself has been lost. The character of the lettering has been described as tenth century, perhaps dating back to the time of Saint Dunstan, and imitating in its turn a sixth-century inscription.[28] Giraldus also identifies Glastonbury with Avalon, reporting that this high ground surrounded by marshlands was called "inis Avallon" or "isle of apples" in the British language, as well as "inis gutrin," "island of glass." He associates Avalon with "Morgan, the noble matron and lady-ruler of those parts," Arthur's close relative, who transported him from the battle of Camlan to her island for healing. This feature of the passage shows Giraldus handing on some aspects of the legend of Arthur's mysterious end, without of course endorsing the politically troublesome notion that Arthur lived on and might reappear.

Modern archaeologists, Leslie Alcock the most prominent among them, have reacted with natural interest to Giraldus and to the link between Glastonbury and Arthur. The damage attendant upon the dissolution of the monasteries in the sixteenth century led to the disappearance of most of the relics Giraldus discusses. Some excavation has at least established the likelihood that Glastonbury was an important

Christian center in the late fifth and sixth centuries. Some distinguished Christians may well have been buried there. Glastonbury's proximity to Cadbury, with its massive fortifications, has also been interpreted as supporting the theory that the historical Arthur lived and died as Giraldus reports.[29]

Early Celtic Sources

Arthur's name occurs first, not in a Latin historical source, but in a Welsh poem. Arthurian literature owes its existence to the tenacious memories, lively imaginations, and patriotic zeal of the Celtic poets, scribes, and prose writers of the seventh through the twelfth centuries who created this influential body of Arthurian material. In a necessarily brisk review of the early Celtic contribution to the development of Arthur's story, interest centers on the new elements it adds, and on the development of the legend throughout this period.

Aneirin, *The Gododdin*. The tantalizing nature of the early Celtic sources on Arthur becomes apparent in the first work to mention Arthur's name, the Welsh elegy *The Gododdin* (ca. 600) ascribed to the poet Aneirin.[30] This poem's subject is not Arthur at all, but the defeat at Catraeth (Catterick in Yorkshire, possibly) of a Celtic force from the region of the Gododdin in southern Scotland. Aneirin is mentioned as a survivor of that conflict. The elegy fulfills one of the classic functions of poetry in early societies, praising and recalling to memory the great deeds of lost heroes, awesome even in defeat.[31] In fact, Aneirin's mention of Arthur is disappointingly incidental. As he describes the feats of Gwawrddur among the warriors of the Gododdin, the poet comments, "He fed black ravens on the wall of the fortress, though he was not Arthur."[32] That is, Gwawrddur supplied corpses for the traditional beasts and birds of prey so often associated with battles in early European epic poetry. Linking the name of the chosen warrior to Arthur unquestionably conveyed a compliment. By the early seventh century Arthur had become a name to conjure with among the Welsh bards. The baldness of the reference itself suggests that Aneirin's audience was expected to catch the allusion with ease. *The Gododdin* also indicates that Arthur now enjoyed a reputation for a fabulous degree of personal prowess. Gwawrddur is being compared to the Arthur Nennius describes as slaying 960 enemies in one battle.[33] Beyond these suggestive inferences, *The Gododdin* does not advance the study of Arthurian narrative.

Arthur in *The Black Book of Carmarthen* and *The Book of Taliesin*. The major thirteenth-century Welsh manuscripts *The Black Book of Carmarthen* and *The Book of Taliesin* both contain a number of important early references to Arthur.[34] In many cases individual poems in these manuscripts have been dated as early as the ninth or tenth centuries. Taliesin, himself the subject of a substantial body of legend, appears in Nennius, and seems to have been a sixth-century poet.[35] His *Elegy for Owain Son of Urien* celebrates one of his contemporaries, Owain, a sixth-century prince of Rheged in north Britain. Owain is of interest to Arthurian scholars because his legend rapidly became associated with Arthur's, as the Arthurian material attracted a surprising number of previously unrelated heroes. While in Taliesin's poem Owain preserves his independence, by the late twelfth century he had become the central figure in Chrétien de Troyes's Arthurian romance *Yvain, or The Knight with the Lion.* In the thirteenth-century Vulgate Cycle and Sir Thomas Malory's *Morte Darthur,* he is ensconced within Arthur's immediate family, as the king's nephew, the son of Arthur's half-sister Morgan le Fay.

The Black Book of Carmarthen preserves the earliest version of an elegy on Geraint the son of Erbin, another sixth-century British chieftain who became a supporter of Arthur in later works.[36] Chrétien's *Erec et Enide* uses the Breton name "Erec" for Geraint, but Alfred, Lord Tennyson, returned to the Welsh form when he retold the story as *Geraint and Enid* in his *Idylls of the King.* In the case of Geraint's elegy, an association with Arthur is visible: both heroes are praised for their feats at the battle of Llongborth (identified tentatively as Langport in Somerset).

The Black Book of Carmarthen also contains "The Stanzas of the Graves," a ninth- or tenth-century poem on the gravesites of famous British heroes, here relocated to Wales presumably to reflect the relocation of the Celts before the advance of the Anglo-Saxons. Although translation is difficult, the poet seems to be reflecting at one point that Arthur's grave is a wonder, something hard to find.[37] Here, then, the legend of Arthur's mysterious disappearance seems to be current. "The Stanzas of the Graves" records the name of Gwalchmai, soon to become identified as Arthur's nephew, Gawain. Also mentioned among the great warriors of Arthur's court are Bedwyr, the future Sir Bedivere; Owain; and March, King Mark of Cornwall in later sources.

The most perplexing of *The Black Book of Carmarthen's* Arthurian references is a fragmentary poem in dialogue, in which Arthur himself is represented as speaking for the first time in literature. Arthur is apparently trying to gain admittance to an unidentified establishment guarded by the porter Glewlwyd Mighty-grip, who in the Welsh prose tale of *Culhwch and Olwen* is Arthur's own porter. Like virtually all porters of medieval literature, Glewlwyd is uncooperative. He elicits from Arthur a long descriptive catalogue of the personages in his retinue that looks forward to the famous list of Arthur's supporters in *Culhwch and Olwen*. In this list the most prominent of Arthur's men is Cei the Fair. Later writers were to see Sir Kay as Arthur's bitter, sharp-tongued seneschal, hardly the most successful knight of the Round Table. For the tenth- or eleventh-century poet at work in this attractive fragment, as well as for the author of *Culhwch and Olwen*, Cei is a powerful fighter, often matched against opponents with supernatural powers. Here, Arthur breaks off in the midst of his praise of Cei just as he is about to relate a battle between his follower and the formidable *cath palug*, the Clawing Cat.[38] In this poem Arthur's court contains warriors like Cei and Bedwyr, together with early Celtic gods. Mabon son of Modron, Manawydan son of Llyr, and Lluch of the Shining Hand all have their prototypes in the Celtic pantheon. Arthur is not merely attracting unrelated historical figures, but gods as well.[39] He is revealed here for the first time at the head of an astonishing court made up of "the best men in the world," as he says himself. Arthur's opponents, too, have been transformed from mere Saxon immigrants to monsters, hags, lions, and other prodigies.

The poem now entitled "The Spoils of Annwn" ("Preiddeu Annwfn") in *The Book of Taliesin* also revels in the fantastic side of the Arthurian legend. It ranks among the most evocative and mysterious of Celtic Arthurian works. Again, the poem is an extremely difficult one to interpret.[40] It seems to be describing an epic journey to the Celtic underworld. *Pridwen*, Arthur's ship, carries him and his men to a series of puzzling and debilitating encounters in the other world. "Three shiploads of Prydwen we went on the sea; / except for seven, none returned from Caer Rigor."[41] Bolland interprets the main advanture as an expedition to rescue the imprisoned Gwair, one of Arthur's men held captive in the deathly realm of Annwn. Like *Culhwch and Olwen*, it shows Arthur, at the head of a redoubtable fighting force, struggling to attain a series of difficult goals.

Arthur in the *Welsh Triads* and the *Mabinogi*.   Two important sources of early Welsh Arthurian material are the very different collections known as *The Triads of the Isle of Britain* and *The Mabinogi* (or more traditionally *The Mabinogion*). The *Triads* are basically lists of groups of three related items or characters, associated as a mnemonic device for the storyteller. They have been edited and extensively discussed by Rachel Bromwich.[42] While triads survive in manuscripts dating from the thirteenth through the fourteenth centuries, the material they contain seems to antedate the manuscripts in which they are preserved. The frustrating feature of the triads is that, in most cases, they are reminders of stories, not the stories themselves. Nowhere else do we have clearer testimony of the richness of early Celtic Arthurian literature, for the most part now lost to us. In the *Triads* we also see Arthur's wife Gwenhywfar for the first time, where she is singled out as even more faithless than the "Three Faithless Wives of the Isle of Britain."[43] This embarrassing triad also points a finger at "Essylt Fair-hair, mistress of Trystan." Evidently the story of Tristan and Isolde the Fair was already in existence, though it was not by any means necessarily connected to Arthur's legend (see Chapter 2). The *Triads* in fact give Arthur three queens named Gwenhwyfar (Bromwich, *Trioedd* no. 56), as well as three mistresses. They blame one of the Gwenhwyfars for starting the disastrous battle of Camlan (Bromwich, *Trioedd* no. 84), though her exact role is not clear. They also record an assault on Arthur's court in Cornwall by Medrawd, and Arthur's revenge (Bromwich, *Trioedd* no. 54). It is clear that many Welsh Arthurian narratives have unfortunately been lost. The *Triads,* more than any other source, make us aware of the nature and extent of our impoverishment.

The most complete Arthurian narratives preserved from early medieval Wales have been associated with the collection of stories known as *The Mabinogi,* or, traditionally but less appropriately, the *Mabinogion*.[44] Though they fall outside the Four Branches of the *Mabinogi* proper, the short prose tales of *Culhwch and Olwen* and *The Dream of Rhonabwy* survive in the same manuscripts and can often be found translated into English in their company.

Of the two, *Culhwch and Olwen* is the better known. It delights and astonishes its modern readers, even in translation, with the earliest full-scale depiction of Arthur's court. Though its two manuscript copies are fourteenth century (1350–1400), *Culhwch and Olwen's* language has been dated as belonging to the late tenth or early eleventh century, so that it may well be the earliest extant Welsh prose text.[45] The narrative combines a number of well-recognized folklore motifs. The framework of the tale is basically that of the "Giant's Daughter," in which the hero, Arthur's young cousin Culhwch, must perform a long series of impossible tasks to win the beautiful Olwen, daughter of Ysbaddadden Chief Giant.[46] Culhwch, surprisingly, takes his name from the pigsty in which his mother bore him. Since the major event of the story is Arthur's hunting of the boar Twrch Trwth across Ireland and Wales, scholars postulate that Celtic mythology concerning an ancient boar-god lies behind *Culhwch*. The real hero of the story, though, is Arthur, to whom Culhwch applies for help. The author's extraordinary catalogue of Arthur's retainers show Cei, Bedwyr, and Gwalchmai once again in attendance on Arthur. The list also bears witness to the Arthurian legend's drawing power, as old Celtic gods, fairy-tale prodigies, and originally independent heroes gravitate to Arthur's court. *Culhwch and Olwen*'s strengths lie in its exuberant detail, comic flair, and flamboyant storytelling. Arthur here displays superhuman generosity, an unfortunate sense of humor, and heroic power at the head of his resourceful and difficult war-band.

The *Dream of Rhonabwy*, perhaps from the thirteenth century, offers a more elegant image of Arthur on the eve of the battle of Mount Badon. The twelfth-century dreamer, Rhonabwy, falls asleep in his own flea-infested and vastly inferior century to experience a vision of Arthur's camp. He observes Owain and Arthur playing chess as Arthur's men skirmish with Owain's ravens. The writer here combines a sophisticated awareness of dream psychology, sensory detail, and social satire in the contrast between Rhonabwy's inadequate contemporaries and the heroic age of Arthur.

Other Celtic works in sixteenth-century manuscripts, the "Dialogue of Arthur and Guinevere," which really involved Guinevere and her abductor Melwas (Meleagant), and the "Dialogue of Arthur and the Eagle," a chiefly religious work, merit attention.[47] Besides these texts, and non-Arthurian materials on the bards Myrddin and Taliesin, the three Welsh romances *Owain (The Lady of the Fountain), Peredur,* and *Geraint and Enid,* deserve mention here, though they will be noted in the next chapter.

Geoffrey of Monmouth's *History of the Kings of Britain*

The *Historia regum Brittaniae (History of the Kings of Britain)* ranks among the most enduringly influential and controversial works of its day, and the twelfth century—the age of Abelard and Eleanor of

Aquitaine—hardly lacked controversial issues. Geoffrey's book draws together the problems and sources discussed earlier in this chapter: Arthur's historicity, the nature of the Latin and Celtic records, and the reliability of local traditions. The *History*'s own historicity is still as debatable as it was when Giraldus Cambrensis described it as a favored resting place of lying demons.[48] Still, Geoffrey's *History* unquestionably gave all later Arthurian works their basic account of Arthur's biography. Later scholarship has been occupied assessing and reassessing the nature of that account ever since it came into circulation.

Meager autobiographical references and documentary evidence enable scholars to outline Geoffrey of Monmouth's own biography. His name suggests that he was either born or educated in the vicinity of Monmouth in southern Wales, though Geoffrey Ashe is inclined to think he may have come from a Breton family. His works certainly reveal his alertness to Breton concerns.[49] His name among the witnesses to a variety of charters places him in the neighborhood of Oxford from 1129 on. There he apparently taught in the schools that preceded the foundation of that university. In these documents he is given the academic title *magister* (Master) and called *Galfridus Arthur* (Geoffrey Arthur), presumably indicating his father's name.[50] Spurred on by his success as a writer and by the patronage of the Bishop of Lincoln, he entered higher orders and was elected Bishop of Saint Asaphs in Wales in 1151. This was hardly a major appointment, and it is unlikely that Geoffrey ever took up his duties in that nest of rebels. He seems to have died in London in 1154–55.

Geoffrey's fame from his lifetime to ours rests on his writings. His three known works all revolve around the story of Arthur. In order of composition, they are, first, the *Prophecies of Merlin (Prophetiae Merlini),* probably composed as early as the 1130s and later incorporated in his second work, the *History of the Kings of Britain*. Study of the alterations Geoffrey made in its dedication allows students of the subject to date the earliest draft of the *History* to about 1136, though some evidence suggests that Geoffrey revised it in the 1140s. Geoffrey's final work, the *Life of Merlin (Vita Merlini),* was completed around 1150. It is a substantial poem combining Welsh accounts of the late sixth-century bard Myrddin and Taliesin (in Geoffrey's Latin, Thelgesinus) with material on Arthur and Vortigern from the *History*.[51]

The *History of the Kings of Britain* is Geoffrey of Monmouth's principal work. Expanding on Nennius, it begins by linking the history of Britain with Virgil's Roman mythology. Brutus, for Geoffrey the

conqueror of the giant-infested isle of Albion, is a grandson of Virgil's
Aeneas, and, through him, a descendant of the Trojan heroes of the
Iliad. Naturally, Britain is renamed in his honor. Geoffrey's descriptions
of the British monarchs who succeeded Brutus were a treasure trove
for later English writers. The stories of Shakespeare's King Lear and
Cymbeline, Milton's Sabrina, and the exploits of Brennius and Belinus
all enliven Geoffrey's narrative. Geoffrey retells the story of Vortigern's
ill-advised invitation to Hengist, and the advent of the Saxons. Here
he inserts his favorite character, the prophet Merlin, the son of an
enterprising demon and a virtuous Welch princess. In Geoffrey, Merlin
replaces Ambrosius as the youth who prophesies before Vortigern. Merlin
goes on to display his magical powers by moving Stonehenge from
Ireland to Salisbury Plain, and engineers the birth of Arthur by magically
bringing together Ambrosius's infatuated brother Uther and the inac-
cessible Duchess Igerna of Cornwall. Here the reader recognizes the
narrative of Arthur's mysterious begetting for the first time in literature.
Other familiar details of Geoffrey's Arthurian scene are Arthur's sword
Caliburn, and the supporting figures of Kay, Bedivere, and Gawain.

In Geoffrey's fifth section, Arthur is crowned, conquers England,
marries Guinevere, and proceeds to enlarge his empire, taking in Ireland,
the Scandinavian countries, and Gaul, where he encounters the western
Roman Empire. These European conquests absorb much of Geoffrey's
interest. They would also attract his aristocratic Norman audience, familiar
with Henry I's Continental campaigns. Geoffrey describes the splendor
of Arthur's court at Caerleon on Usk, remodeled to suit twelfth-century
taste with tournaments and other military games, liturgical ceremonies,
and separate banquets for men and women. Arthur then returns to
Gaul to take up the challenge of the Roman procurator Lucius, who
has demanded his submission. On the way he engages the horrific giant
of Mont-Saint-Michel in single combat. Triumphant in his second
Continental foray, Arthur is poised on the verge of a journey to Rome,
presumably to accept the title of emperor, when he is summoned home
to Britain to confront his nephew Mordred. Tha usurper's attempt to
seize Queen Guinevere and the throne leads to Arthur's costly final
victory at the river Camel in Cornwall. Geoffrey's Arthur disappears
from history at this point, borne off to the mysterious isle of Avalon
for healing. Geoffrey of Monmouth then continues his narrative of
British rulers as far as the seventh-century reign of Cadwallader.

Debate over the sources Geoffrey of Monmouth employed for his
History has embroiled historical and literary scholars on and off since

the twelfth century. It has been established that Geoffrey's style and taste for epic effect, owes much to his reading in the classics, notably Virgil and Juvenal.[52] He was also acquainted with most of the Latin historical sources discussed earlier in this chapter, as well as with the work of his medieval contemporaries. The greatest controversy centers around Geoffrey's claim to a lost source, the "British book" shown to him by his friend Walter, archdeacon of Oxford, who was certainly not a fictional character. Most probably, his as yet undiscovered book, brought "from Britain," or perhaps "from Brittany," "ex Britanniae" would have been Breton rather than Welsh. Geoffrey asserts that it gives him privileged information, and warns other historians, who do not have access to this authoritative volume, not to meddle with the British kings.[53] Modern scholarly reactions to Geoffrey's announcements range from the school of thought that sees Geoffrey, like many other medieval authors, giving his work an extra veneer of authority by bestowing on it an imaginary and suitably ancient pedigree. At the opposite extreme, Geoffrey Ashe asserts the probability that Geoffrey of Monmouth did have some sort of lost Breton record of Arthur's fifty-century Continental career, which is echoed in the *Life of St. Goeznovius.*[54]

What, finally, is the effect of Geoffrey of Monmouth's account of Arthur? The *History of the Kings of Britain,* in spite of the quibbles of Giraldus Cambrensis, gave Arthur historical status and an historical context in the international learned language of the Middle Ages. Geoffrey of Monmouth brought Arthur to the center of the twelfth-century stage. The Arthur he celebrates travels well beyond local Welsh and Breton concerns to participate in the affairs of Europe at large. Geoffrey's Arthur may be modeled after Charlemagne, or Alexander.[55] He may also have been specially tailored to appeal to the Norman aristocracy to whom Geoffrey addressed his work. Robert, Duke of Gloucester, King Stephen of England, and Waleran, Count of Mellant, all receive dedicatory mention in various manuscripts, as does Geoffrey's own bishop, Robert of Chertsey.[56] Arthur's conquests span the Norman sphere of influence, from their Scandinavian point of departure as Viking raiders to the great Norman conquests in France and England. The magical events of his begetting and disappearance give Arthur's biography the ambiance of classical epic, though they also unquestionably owe much to the Celtic imaginations of writers like the author of *Culhwch and Olwen.* Geoffrey's Arthur is a general with imperial ambitions, as well as a formidable warrior and leader. His court replaces the flamboyant marvels of the Celtic scene with a more ordered majesty. Still, it would be ridiculous to suggest that Geoffrey of Monmouth had diminished the element of wonder in Arthur's biography. The effectiveness of his work lies in his ability to fuse history and marvel, fact and imagination, into an indissoluble whole.

Successors of Geoffrey of Monmouth: *De ortu Waluuanii,* Wace, Layamon

Three followers of Geoffrey of Monmouth bridge the gap between the *History of the Kings of Britain* and the world of the twelfth-century vernacular romances. Wace's French *Romance of Brutus (Roman de Brut)* and Layamon's Middle English *Brut* show Geoffrey of Monmouth's influence at the start of two new vernacular traditions, while the *Rise of Gawain (De ortu Waluuanii)* represents a continuation of Geoffrey of Monmouth's Arthurian interests in Latin.

The Rise of Gawain, Nephew of Arthur (De ortu Waluuanii). The *Rise of Gawain* has been dated anywhere from the late twelfth to the later thirteenth century. Its Latin prose account of the adventures of Arthur's nephew Gawain connects directly with Geoffrey of Monmouth's depiction of Arthur. Gawain's mother is Arthur's sister Anna, the name given to her in Geoffrey's *History*. Born out of wedlock, Gawain is shipped off to the Roman emperor for military training, and receives his first command among the empire's mounted troops. He distinguishes himself somewhat anachronistically in a duel with a Persian warrior at the siege of Jerusalem, after which the narrative concludes with Gawain's return to join Arthur in battle against a troublesome wave of raiders to the north. Gawain's prowess leads to a satisfying revelation of his true identity and his admission to Arthur's court. The principal modern authority on the work, its editor, Mildred Leake Day, notes that there are some attractive reasons for accepting John Bale's attribution of the *Rise of Gawain* to Robert of Torigni, abbot of Mont-Saint-Michel from 1154 to 1186, the librarian who introduced the astonished historian Henry of Huntington to Geoffrey's *History of the Kings of Britain.*[57]

Wace. On the fringes of the romance one of the most appealing figures is Wace, a Norman poet of considerable talent, born around 1110 on the channel island of Jersey. His *Romance of Brutus (Roman de Brut)* completed in 1155 and dedicated to Queen Eleanor of Aquitaine, follows Geoffrey of Monmouth's *History*. It adds significantly to the body of Arthurian motifs, perhaps because of contact with the Celtic oral tradition.[58] The Round Table is only the most famous Arthurian item to be introduced in the *Roman de Brut*. Wace is the first to comment directly on Breton stories as sources of Arthurian material. He also remarks upon the Bretons' continuing faith in Arthur's return. Wace is notable for his instincts as an on-the-spot reporter. His own travels in England may be reflected in the geographical details of his Arthurian narrative. In his later work, the *Romance of Rollo (Roman de Rou)*, he tells us of his disappointing visit to the Breton forest of Brocéliande, famed as the site of Merlin's eternal imprisonment in a hollow oak tree, as well as other marvels of faerie. "A fool I went," says Wace ruefully, "a fool I came back." In view of the many charms of Wace's style, it is hardly surprising that his accessible French version of Geoffrey of Monmouth attained wide currency in manuscript; eighteen complete copies survive.[59] Its impact can be traced in the work of most major contributors to French Arthurian romance, among them Wace's contemporaries Chrétien de Troyes and Marie de France, and the thirteenth-century compilers of the Vulgate Cycle of Arthurian prose romances.

Layamon, *Brut*. With Layamon's *Brut* the long history of Arthurian literature in English begins. Layamon's work also ranks among the first substantial compositions in Middle English to survive. Its linguistic and literary importance cannot be overestimated. In many ways, Layamon is singular. A priest living at Arley Regis in Worcester, he probably wrote in the final decade of the twelfth or the early thirteenth century. The two extant manuscripts of his work, British Library manuscripts Cotton Caligula A.ix. and Cotton Otho C.xiii., are dated at fifty years to a century later.[60] Layamon takes his narrative largely from Wace, though he claims to use Bede's *Ecclesiastical History* and a so far unidentifiable third source as supplements. Beyond some possible Celtic details, Layamon's principal contribution to Arthurian literature lies in his character as a writer. His poem attempts to preserve the main effects of Old English alliterative form, though in Layamon the resulting methods have been characterized as idiosyncratic.[61] But if its method is difficult to classify, the power of Layamon's work itself cannot be denied. Where Wace was courtly, Layamon's Arthurian world is savage in its violence, and described in the most direct imagery. Its forceful dialogue and dramatic effectiveness make Layamon's *Brut* unforgettable. The English Arthurian tradition clearly begins with a masterpiece, if an unexpected one.

Critics have asked why a descendant of the historical Arthur's Saxon enemies, writing in a Saxon poetic mode, should celebrate this British hero.[62] One might equally well wonder why the French, another people supposedly conquered by Arthur, should take any interest in his legend. Native epic heroes were hardly lacking in either society. The mystery of Arthur's popularity deepens here, in the twelfth century. What factors in the story of Arthur made that narrative so adept at crossing cultural boundaries? Geoffrey of Monmouth's Latin *History of the Kings of Britain,* with its claims of historical truth and its international language, certainly remains a key work for the study of this problem. The next chapter, which follows Arthur's progress into the new world of chivalric romance, further explores the issue of Arthur's popularity.

Chapter Two
Medieval Arthurian Romances

The inventive twelfth century seems an entirely appropriate location for Geoffrey of Monmouth's astonishing combination of Arthurian legend and history. Indeed, that era contributed still more to the story of Arthur. This chapter discusses the alliance forged, first in France, and then across Europe over the next three centuries between the "matter of Britain," now one of the three proverbial categories of heroic narrative, and the rapidly developing species of vernacular fiction that we call the chivalric romance.

Of all the artistic forms into which the Arthurian legend has been recast over the centuries, it seems to remain most closely linked to the romance. The long prehistory of the genre stretches back to the adventure romances of the classical era, while its influence continues to be felt in many twentieth-century novels.[1] The twelfth-century romances took their name from the fact that they were written in the romance vernacular language French, rather than in Latin. They obviously differed in plot structure and preoccupation from the vernacular epics of previous centuries—*The Song of Roland,* or in English, *Beowulf.* Where those poems depicted the warriors of the heroic past attaining glory through death in battle, the romances turned to new interests: love, the achievement of social rank through military prowess, the ethics of combat, the young man's or young woman's quest for identity. It is tempting to define the romance as the *Bildungsroman* of the Middle Ages. Both the French historian Georges Duby and the English critic Derek Brewer suggest that romances were first invented to please a youthful audience, providing fantasy and instruction for the young and unsettled men and women of the twelfth-century courts, in particular younger sons without land holdings, the *juventes.*[2] The earliest romances were written in verse, but the thirteenth century saw the rise of prose romances. In either case, hearing or reading a romance was a social event for both courtly and popular audiences; a taste for romances cuts across the social scale, from monarch to artisan.[3]

Chrétien de Troyes

It is appropriate to begin the study of the romance with perhaps its most famous poet, Chrétien de Troyes. Shortly after the death of Geoffrey of Monmouth in 1154–55, Chrétien set to work transposing the Arthurian story into the new form of the romance. Very little information concerning his biography has been amassed by the many scholars who have investigated his work. He was apparently active as a poet from the late 1150s until 1190, which could be the year of his death. His own name and dialect link him to the city of Troyes in Champagne. The dedications of his works associate him with the court of Marie, countess of Champagne, the daughter of Eleanor of Aquitaine by her first marriage to King Louis VII of France, and with Philip, count of Flanders (d. 1191).[4] In the forty years of his career as a poet, Chrétien wrote the five Arthurian romances that still over-shadow all later French works in this genre: *Erec et Enide; Cligès; Lancelot, or The Knight of the Cart; Yvain, or The Knight with the Lion;* and *Perceval, or The Story of the Grail,* which was frustratingly left incomplete in 1190. In these major narrative poems Chrétien fixed many of the patterns that later authors were to follow. Here we find the Holy Grail, the adventures of a solitary knight errant on his quest, the sharp-tongued maiden who so often taunts him, and the vexing question of "courtly love."

Chrétien removes Arthur completely from the epic tradition of Geoffrey of Monmouth and his followers. His focus is on Arthur's knights, not on Arthur himself. Each of his romances is centered on a new hero with new moral and psychological problems to solve. The Arthur who hovers in the background of Chrétien's five principal works cannot even be described as a positive figure. Like the king on the modern chessboard, he seems almost immobilized.[5] *Yvain* begins with Arthur nodding off to sleep. In *Lancelot* Arthur allows his queen to be kidnapped, and makes only a feeble attempt to search for her: he is bullied by Kay and cuckolded by Lancelot. Critics have explained this drastic fall in Arthur's status, a phenomenon known generally as "epic degeneration," by pointing out that Chrétien was not writing for the king of France but for his vassals, a group of independent-minded aristocrats with negative views of central royal authority. Their ideal king might well resemble Chrétien's Arthur.

Chrétien's influence on Arthurian literature carries well beyond his treatment of Arthur himself. He confronts many of the most complex problems that have preoccupied Arthurian writers up to the present day. In his earliest surviving romance, *Erec et Enide (Erec and Enide)*, Chrétien investigates the conflict between knighthood and marriage. Where many more typical romances end with a knight marrying his lady, in *Erec et Enide*, the young hero's winning and wedding of his true love only ends the first stage of the narrative. Erec is rudely awakened from his long honeymoon when he overhears his bride, Enide, lamenting that his passion for her has diverted him from the pursuit of chivalry. His furious response is to drag her out on a quest with him. Readers from the Middle Ages on have in turn lamented Erec's cruelty and Enide's acquiescence as unpleasant features of the plot. This problem is inherent in the story, and by no means eliminated in Tennyson's nineteenth-century version of the same tale. Nevertheless, as Chrétien works out his story, Erec both regains his chivalric reputation and learns to value Enide's love, perhaps most when he is in danger of losing her to a marauding baron. Arthur's role here is peripheral; his court provides the background from which Erec sets out on his first quest, the hunt in the forest that leads him unexpectedly to Enide.

From the first, Chrétien establishes himself as a poet of consummate skill. His deft comic touch and musical choice of language were hardly apparent in the older English translations of his works. A number of recent translations, however, have brought twentieth-century readers closer to appreciating Chrétien as a poet.[6]

In *Cligès*, his next romance, Chrétien took up the problem of the queen in love with one of her husband's knights. This love triangle was to provide the tension in the two great Arthurian love stories of Tristan and Isolde and Lancelot and Guinevere. Chrétien's extant works do not take up the originally non-Arthurian story of Tristan, though he does refer to it explicitly in *Cligès*. His list of his own works in *Cligès*, many of them lost, includes "King Mark and Isolde the Fair."[7] Norris J. Lacy in fact discusses *Cligès* as a variant of *Tristan*. Here Fénice, the heroine, escapes from Isolde's predicament by the back door. By feigning death, she is able to free herself from her unwanted marriage and live happily, if immorally, with the knight of her affections, Cligès— not as immorally as Isolde, be it said.[8] Again, Arthur's court provides a stopping-off point for the characters, rather than a major setting; the same observation may be made of all Chrétien's romances. Arthur's court stands in the background, providing the basic standard against which the main characters are measured. Sometimes they sink below the moral level of the Round Table, and at other times they are expected to soar beyond it. Chrétien's eye, as he depicts Arthur and his knights, is never uncritical.

Chrétien's three remaining works take him into still more difficult territory. Two, *Lancelot* and *Yvain,* are approximately contemporary with one another. *Le Chevalier de la charrette (Lancelot, or The Knight of the Cart)* is remarkable as one of the earliest appearances of that hero in literature. Chrétien brings him on the scene, he says, at the command of his lady, Marie de Champagne. He is the mysteriously unnamed knight riding to the rescue of the kidnapped Guinevere, with whom he is desperately in love. Chrétien has a good deal of fun here with the foibles of lovers. The psychological convolutions of Lancelot and Guinevere's monologues are at once credible and entertainingly exaggerated. After humiliating his hero immediately by forcing him to ride in a cart like a criminal to the gallows, Chrétien rehabilitates him through a series of further trials, culminating when he crosses the Sword Bridge into the forbidden land where Guinevere is held prisoner. The fact that Guinevere initially rejects him, not for riding in the cart, but for hesitating an instant before getting in, enforces the point that society's judgments and those of love differ radically. Lancelot does free Guinevere, and sleep with her, only to see her charged with adultery, from which he must defend her in a second duel with her abductor, Meleagant. Treacherously imprisoned by his enemy, Lancelot is freed to fight in a tournament at Arthur's court, imprisoned again, and finally escapes to defeat Meleagant once more. Chrétien did not finish his romance, but apparently passed it to a certain Geoffroy de Leigni to complete. Chrétien also fails to address the moral issue of Guinevere's adultery, though he does palliate the situation by enfeebling Arthur to an almost ludicrous extent and depriving Lancelot of any noticeable relationship with his king.

Chrétien's Lancelot is a classic "courtly lover." His total devotion to Arthur's queen gives expression to the twelfth century's exploration of a new code of elegant courtship. Since Gaston Paris invented the term *courtly love (amour courtois)* and C. S. Lewis defined it in *The Allegory of Love,* the nature and existence of an aristocratic medieval ideal of love has been much debated. Chrétien's *Lancelot* lies at the center of the debate, because of its subject matter and because of its connection with the court of Marie de Champagne, where Andreas Capellanus (Andrew the Chaplain) also wrote his *De arte honeste amandi* giving rules for twelfth-century aristocratic lovers. Andreas's solemn pronouncements that love and marriage are mutually exclusive, that abject servitude is the proper attitude of a knight to his lady, and his descriptions of the symptoms of love—sleeplessness, loss of appetite, a discolored complexion—have been accepted at face value by some critics. Others regard the whole composition as an unrecognized spoof of Ovid's *Ars amatoria*.[9] Whatever Andreas Capellanus's motives may have been, his book remains a source for the study of attitudes to love in medieval romance. It certainly seems that some sort of literary or social games related to love were played at Marie de Champagne's court; it also seems fair to say that from the troubadors on the concept of an idealized love, of human passion exalted to the level of an alternative religion, provides a major theme for the authors of romances. A successful knight, as of Chrétien's day, was expected to be a devoted lover as well as a powerful warrior and a virtuous Christian. The stresses of these sometimes incompatible requirements provide much of the tension in the later romances.

Le Chevalier au lion (Yvain, or The Knight with the Lion) is one of Chrétien's most successful works, perhaps because it does not take on the complex issues of *Lancelot*. Here again, Chrétien studies the relationship between chivalry and love. In this case, Yvain wins his lady after killing her husband in a duel by the magic fountain he guards. He then leaves her for a year of knightly exploits in the company of his friend Gawain, only to forget all about his promise to his bride. When her messenger denounces him before King Arthur's court, Yvain expresses his shame by running mad in the forest. Reduced to nonentity, he must regain his chivalric reputation and restore his marriage through a series of escalating adventures that are also tests of character. The lion who helps him in this quest has been explained symbolically as some moral or religious quality, but no explanation is really needed. The lion is a charming character in his own right, and the relationship between him and his knight is one of the best features of the romance.

Le Roman de Perceval (Le conte du graal) (Perceval, or The Story of the Grail), which Chrétien left unfinished at his death, became the first of a long line of grail romances focused around that most mysterious of Arthurian objects. When the romance opens, Chrétien's unsophisticated hero, Perceval, has been brought up in the forest by his mother, who has sheltered him from all knowledge of knighthood in order to preserve him from this deadly profession. Naturally, on his first glimpse of knights in armor, he rushes off to become a knight himself. Perceval's naiveté involves him in a series of faux pas, or worse. At King Arthur's court he makes a boisterous entrance reminiscent of Culhwch's, and kills the knight who has challenged the court to a joust. A kindly nobleman, Gornemanz, teaches him some basic rules of courtly behavior. This new knowledge, unfortunately, only leads to his humiliation at the magical Grail Castle, where Perceval, entertained sumptuously by the wounded Fisher King, sees a mysterious procession centered around a large dish or "graal" containing a single mass wafer, and a bleeding spear. Perceval is now too polite to ask the natural question that would have ended his host's suffering. *Perceval* breaks off as its hero, denounced at court by a truly repulsive damsel for his omission, sets out on a quest to repair his fault, clearly still with much to learn. Four continuators of the romance provided it with additional adventures of Perceval and Gawain, as well as with two different endings. For the continuing history of the grail itself, readers must turn to later authors.

Where did Chrétien find the idea of the grail? What was it? Writers of the next generation differ widely in their depictions and explanations of the grail. Chrétien's is clearly a dish or platter, one suitable for serving a large fish, he tells us. Like the magical cauldrons of Celtic legend, it can function as a kind of "horn of plenty," providing favorite dishes for an assembled company. Such a cauldron is listed among the many extraordinary objects Arthur had to collect for Culhwch. Stories of raids on the Celtic Other World often involve the capture of such magical treasures. R. S. Loomis has explored Chrétien's possible Celtic sources in detail. The grail does seem to have some pagan Celtic analogues. Chrétien's successors, notably the Burgundian poet Robert de Boron, were to portray the grail as a christian relic, identifying it as the chalice used at the Last Supper, the cup used to catch the drops of Christ's blood at the deposition from the cross, or both. In later works, the grail retains its ancient power to supply food to its followers, but becomes linked to Christian theology through the cult of the Holy Blood and the doctrine of transubstantiation.[10]

It seems entirely characteristic of Chrétien that he should leave his readers by introducing them to one of the chief mysteries of Arthurian legend: he is a poet as celebrated for his enigmas as for his innovative power. Through his five romances Chrétien de Troyes greatly expanded the boundaries of Arthurian legend. His characters learn the nature of their world, and the moral qualities they need to live in it. Chrétien's readers, in their turn, learn something of the author's sympathetic understanding of the human spirit.

The European Tradition

After Chrétien the extraordinary proliferation of the Arthurian romance has presented a major challenge to scholars concerned with its investigation. As a result, some works of great merit have been unfortunately neglected; many specialized studies are available, but few comprehensive investigations of the field. This chapter makes no claim to exhaustive coverage. It begins by discussing the French Vulgate Cycle of prose romances, the thirteenth century's consolidation of scattered Arthurian narratives in a massive history of the Round Table. From there it presents a compact overview of the European tradition of Arthurian chivalric romances, with special attention to the story of Tristan and the grail romances. The main principle of selection here is to stress those works most important in their own right, and those of greatest influence on later English Arthurian literature. The final section of the chapter focuses more closely on the English Arthurian romances, especially *Sir Gawain and the Green Knight* and the alliterative *Morte Arthure* and stanzaic *Morte Arthur*.

The series of five thirteenth-century French prose romances known today as the Vulgate Cycle gave its multitude of readers a connected history of the Arthurian world and the Holy Grail, linking the events of the New Testament with the chivalrous adventures of Arthur's Britain.

The unknown author or authors' choice of prose rather than verse for this ambitious undertaking was almost certainly influenced by the popularity of the new vernacular prose histories. In Geoffrey of Monmouth's day, narrative history or pseudohistory was properly written in Latin. Where many verse romances offered at least the possibility of their memorization for performance by wandering minstrels, the voluminous prose romance was tied to the manuscript page. This did not necessarily limit the size of its audience or confine it to the literate. Reading aloud to a group of listeners at court or in a wealthy household was a regular source of entertainment and means of transmission. Many surviving manuscripts are lavish display copies, with illustrations to enhance their appeal. The possession of such a book does imply substantial resources on the part of the owner.[11]

Precursors of the Vulgate Cycle: Robert de Boron. Primary credit for the concept of a comprehensive grail history must be given to Robert de Boron, a Burgundian poet who seems to have written

early in the thirteenth century. His reference to an association of some
kind with the crusader Gautier of Montbéliard (d. 1212) suggests he
came from the nearby village of Boron, and also hints at a date for
his work. Robert's only complete poem to survive, *Joseph d'Arimathie*
(*Joseph of Arimathea*), traces the grail, here used by Christ at the Last
Supper and then by Joseph of Arimathea to collect Christ's blood after
the Crucifixion. The grail sustains Joseph in prison, after which it is
carried abroad by Joseph and his family. In a final miraculous event,
Joseph is instructed by the Holy Spirit to arrange a grail table in
commemoration of the Last Supper. There the chaste take their places
and are rewarded by ineffable ecstasy; those guilty of lechery are excluded,
and the earth gapes to receive the rash sinner who attempts to sit at
the table. Robert ends *Joseph* by sketching in the future history of the
grail. It is to be taken into the west by Joseph's brother-in-law, Bron
or Hebron, the Rich Fisher, presumably to the "vales of Avalon,"
Glastonbury.

Clearly Robert planned to continue his account of the grail's travels.
His *Merlin,* however, skips over the adventures of the grail bearers to
narrate the life of Merlin, who becomes the prophet of the grail. Robert's
Merlin breaks off abruptly in its one surviving manuscript. The Vulgate
Cycle prose *Merlin,* to be discussed shortly, preserves Robert's narrative.
Two manuscripts give us a longer series, connecting prose *Joseph* and
Merlin romances based on Robert's poems with a prose romance of
Perceval—the *Didot Perceval,* named for a previous owner of B.N. MS.
nouv. aq. 4166—and a prose *Mort Artu (Death of Arthur).* This
grouping may have been envisioned by Robert de Boron himself, by
a continuator, or only by the compilers of these manuscripts.[12]

His critics have explored Robert de Boron's dependence on a variety
of sources, from the Bible and Christian apocrypha on. Like Geoffrey
of Monmouth, he too claims to be using a lost book. Others have
deplored his stylistic defects. Still, Robert de Boron can be credited at
least with the articulation of a sacramental prehistory for the grail. His
grand attempt to link the Round Table and the table of the Last
Supper led the chivalric adventures of Arthur's knights towards a new
spiritual dimension that was to prove immensely attractive to later
authors.

From the spark of Robert de Boron's history of the grail, the thirteenth
century was to develop a series of prose romances mapping out a vast
web of chivalric and mystical adventures for Arthur and his knights.
Much of this French material has never been tapped by later Arthurian

works. It remains an enticing labyrinth of sources for future exploration. Unluckily for the English-speaking reader, much still remains untranslated, though major sections of the fifteenth-century *Morte Darthur* of Sir Thomas Malory based on this material give us some idea of its fascination.

Prose romances of the Vulgate Cycle. The five Vulgate Cycle romances are: first, the *Story of the Holy Grail (Estoire del Saint Graal)*; second, the prose *Merlin* derived from Robert de Boron's lost poem on that subject, and its sequel, the *Suite du Merlin,* which might be translated *Merlin Continued.* Third comes a voluminous prose *Lancelot;* fourth, the *Quest of the Holy Grail (Queste del Saint Graal);* and finally, the *Death of Arthur (Mort Artu).* The most recent scholarship on the subject identifies the first two works, paradoxically, as the last to be composed; still later authors attached their own prose romances to the cycle or modeled other extended prose romances after it.

Speculation over the Vulgate Cycle's origins points toward a workshop of some kind in Champagne, and suggests that several different authors were at work under supervision of a single planner, perhaps around 1215–30. None of the writers or patrons connected with this massive project has yet been identified.[13]

The bulk of the Vulgate Cycle is occupied by the prose *Lancelot.* This extended narration of Lancelot's adventures begins with the hero's birth as the son of the beleaguered King Ban of Benouic, a vaguely defined kingdom somewhere in western France. After his father's death, Lancelot is spirited away by the Lady of the Lake to be educated along with his cousins Lionel and Bors in her palace concealed beneath the mirage of a lake. Lancelot is knighted by Arthur, the anomalous features of this event being the Lady of the Lake's lecture on the nature of knighthood and the fact that Lancelot receives his sword not from Arthur but from Guinevere. Lancelot's love for Guinevere is furthered by his friend Galehaut, who brings them together. At the same time, Arthur's affair with the enchantress Camille, and his acceptance of a false Guinevere in place of the real one help to justify the lovers' adultery.

Certainly one major interest of *Lancelot* is the depiction of this most famous or infamous chivalric love affair, with incidents drawn from Chrétien and other early Lancelot traditions.[14] *Lancelot* also looks forward to the quest of the Holy Grail, as it narrates the begetting of the supreme grail knight, Galaad (Galahad), whose father is Lancelot and his mother the daughter of King Pelles of Corbenic, the keeper of the grail. Lancelot is of course completely faithful to Guinevere, but is deluded by means of a magic potion into mistaking Elaine of Corbenic for the queen. We also see the beginning of the end: Arthur commits unintentional incest with his half-sister Morgause, and begets his slayer, Mordred; Lancelot paints incriminating murals of his affair with Guinevere on the walls of Morgan le Fay's dungeon, which are left for Arthur to see in the *Mort Artu*.

As its critics have observed, the prose *Lancelot*'s strength lies in its acute psychological observation and deceptively tight planning. Unlike many of its successors, *Lancelot* observes a strict chronology. Quests are deftly intertwined with one another using the technique of "interlace" *(entrelacement)* to maintain suspense and enhance thematic parallels between the adventures. The romance's weakness lies in its extreme length and repetition of incidents. Even a thirteenth-century love of patterning cannot justify the author's ascribing three episodes of insanity to Lancelot.[15]

In the *Quest of the Holy Grail* the reader moves into an austere monastic world. The virgin knight Galahad's arrival at the Round Table provokes a tantalizing materialization of the grail in Arthur's hall, and sends the assembled knights on a quest to find that elusive relic. Galahad's ability to sit in the Siege Perilous and draw a sword from a stone have already marked him out as the chosen grail knight, and in fact he experiences very few adventures, since he is destined by God to succeed. Regrettably, the grail's appearance has also attracted a host of most unsuitable questers. At the other end of the moral spectrum, Gawain, Lionel, and other unworthy knights blunder across the landscape slaughtering one another by mistake. Between these extremes, Bohort (Bors) and Perceval also achieve the grail after passing through a series of temptations. The laborious Bohort, Lancelot's cousin, perhaps suggests what Lancelot might have been; he, too, is an unwed father, but otherwise chaste. Perceval is still an innocent triumphing through faith rather than through wisdom, though here he is a virgin like Galahad; other romances, including Chrétien's, represent him as a married man. Scholars have suggested that he lost his position as principal grail knight because the author of the *Quest* wanted a more idealized hero. Lancelot presents an even greater problem. Under the essentially antichivalric system of values of the *Quest*, Lancelot stands condemned for his sin with Guinevere, the same sin that had made him the greatest knight and lover of the prose *Lancelot*. In the *Quest*, Lancelot is browbeaten by a succession of sermonizing hermits, repents in agony, and achieves a partial vision of the grail. Pauphilet, Gilson, and their successors have demonstrated the extent to which the *Quest* is permeated by the ideals of Cistercian monasticism, with chastity at the head of the list. Here the Holy Grail symbolizes the grace of God, manifested in the Eucharist. The final mystery witnessed by Galahad before his death is that of the True Presence.[16]

The *Mort Artu* moves back to Arthur's court to retell the story of the king's fall, now complicated by the revelation of Lancelot's affair with Guinevere. The *Mort Artu* moves inexorably from Lancelot's relapse into adultery with Guinevere after his renunciation during the grail quest, through the death of the fair maid of Escalot from unrequited love for him and the appearance of her corpse bearing an explanatory letter at King Arthur's court. Guinevere's wracking fits of jealousy, Arthur's hesitation, and Lancelot's guilt are all depicted effectively, as the narrative approaches the final betrayal of the lovers, thanks to Lancelot's paintings and Gawain's brother Agravain. Lancelot kills Gawain's innocent brother Gaheriet in his rescue of Guinevere from the stake. At this point the *Mort Artu* connects with the chronology of Arthur's life that had been standard since Geoffrey of Monmouth. It does this by carrying the war between Arthur and Lancelot to Lancelot's lands in France: Guinevere has been returned to her husband by papal mandate, but Gawain insists on revenge for his brother's death. Arthur is then attacked by the Romans and battles them as in the *History of the Kings of Britain*. He hears of Mordred's rebellion, returns to Britain for the last battle, and, mortally wounded, orders his knight Griflet to throw Escalibor, his magic sword, back into the lake before being carried off by a fairy barge for burial in the Black Chapel. Guinevere dies a nun. Lancelot returns to England to take vengeance on Mordred's sons, and dies after a period of austerity as a hermit. (In a few manuscripts Lancelot and Guinevere are granted a last interview at Guinevere's convent: this scene was later memorably reenacted in the Middle English stanzaic *Morte Arthur* and in Malory.)[17] Indeed, throughout the *Mort Artu* English and American readers are on familiar ground. The Vulgate account of Arthur's fall and the tragic destruction of the Round Table became the primary source for most English-speaking authors.

To this bloc of three prose romances was later added the *Estoire del Saint Graal (Story of the Holy Grail)*, which told of the prehistory of the grail, Lancelot's lineage, and the Christianization of Britain, closely paralleling Robert de Boron. Robert's *Joseph* may be its direct source, or the two may both derive from a common original, perhaps Robert's lost great book of the grail.[18]

A second addition, the Vulgate *Merlin,* begins as a prose version of Robert de Boron's *Merlin,* but diverges from it to connect with the Vulgate Cycle. Merlin, here again, is the child of a demon and a pious lady. The romance's account of early British history seems to be loosely adapted from some vague reminiscence of Geoffrey of Monmouth. Merlin assists the two British kings Pandragon and his brother Uterpendragon. He connives at the nocturnal visit of Uter to the unsuspecting Ygerne, and watches over their son, young Arthur, up to the point when he takes the sword from the anvil to assert his claim to the British throne. One major preoccupation of this romance is the presentation of the Round Table as the third in a series of sacred tables, linked to the table of the Last Supper and the grail table. Its characterization of Merlin as a mischief maker is also a prototype for future versions.[19]

A still later sequel to the Vulgate *Merlin* describes the young King Arthur's struggles to unify his kingdom in the face of a hostile aristocracy. It also chronicles the early adventures of Gawain, battles against the Saxons and against the Romans in France. Merlin remains an important presiding figure until he is deceived by Viviane and imprisoned forever in the forest of Brocéliande.

The *Suite du Merlin* and the "Post–Vulgate Cycle." A different continuation of *Merlin* surviving in a few manuscripts is known today as the *Suite du Merlin (Merlin Continued).* It gives us, again, the early adventures of Arthur, as well as Gawain, King Pellinore, and the doomed knight Balain, who fights to the death with his beloved brother. This second continuation of *Merlin* has been studied in depth by Eugène Vinaver and Fanni Bogdanow as the most probable source of Sir Thomas Malory's books 1–4. It connects with the *Story of the Holy Grail* and a post-Vulgate *Mort Artu* in a new cycle, the "Post–Vulgate Cycle," showing again the thirteenth century's fondness for comprehensive systems.[20]

Beyond the Vulgate and post–Vulgate cycles, a daunting number of additional Arthurian romances, the majority of them written in the late twelfth to the mid-thirteenth century, testify to Arthur's vogue during that period. They can be roughly grouped according to subject matter. One important category is that of the Tristan romances, originally non-Arthurian but later drawn into the orbit of the Round Table. A second group concerns the grail, continuing the Perceval story first visible in

Chrétien's romance. A third category focuses around Gawain: the French Gauvain (Gawain) romances have been studied in detail by Keith Busby.[21] Finally, many Continental Arthurian romances defy classification, and must remain "miscellaneous."

The Tristan romances. The progress of the immortal love story of Tristan and Isolde in the Middle Ages might be described as a gradual drift toward the Arthurian legend. Originally, Tristan seems to have been an independent Celtic hero, like Owain (Yvain) or Geraint (Erec), whether factual or fictional. The name Tristan derived from the Pictish Drust or Drustan, while tradition associates Castle Dore and the area of Fowey in Cornwall with the Tristan story. Although a Tristan confronts Arthur in a Welsh triad, "Three Powerful Swineherds," the early Tristan romances remain independent entities.[22] By about 1160 some complete version of Tristan's adventures must have been popular in Europe, though regrettably most of the early verse romances of Tristan exist today only as fragments, while some, like Chrétien's story of Mark and Isolde, have been lost altogether.

Among the short narrative poems she based on the work of Breton storytellers, the twelfth-century poet Marie de France included an episode from the Tristan legend. Her "Lay of the Honeysuckle" ("Lai du chèvrefeuille") describes an illicit tryst between Tristan and Isolde in the forest. Like most of Marie's pieces, it is a charming incident, presupposing knowledge of a Tristan narrative much like those we know today.[23]

One early version of the complete Tristan romance is represented by Béroul's fragment of around 1190, and in a German translation by Eilhart von Oberge (ca. 1170). A second more courtly retelling by Thomas of Britain (1155–85) has been pieced together from eight manuscript fragments. Thomas was the main source used by the Middle High German poet Gottfried von Strassburg, whose unfinished *Tristan* is one of the universally acknowledged masterpieces of medieval literature. The Old Norse saga of Tristan preserves what seems to be a complete translation of Thomas's work. Many references in medieval and early Renaissance Italian literature indicate that the Tristan story was extremely popular in Italy as well.[24]

The basic story of Tristan, reconstructed from the fragmentary romances that survive, begins with the love story of Tristan's parents, the king of Lyonesse and the sister of King Mark of Cornwall. After his parents die tragically, Tristan is brought up by his tutor, Governal, becoming accomplished as a harper and hunter as well as a knight.

Accepted at his uncle Mark's court, he defeats Morholt of Ireland, a
veteran warrior, in a duel over the tribute Ireland demands from Cornwall.
Desperately wounded by Morholt's poisoned weapons, he is set adrift
in a ship. By good fortune or astute planning, he arrives in Ireland,
where he assumes the name Tantris and is healed by Morholt's niece,
the princess Isolde la Blonde (Isolde the Fair). On a subsequent visit
as an emissary for Mark to ask for Isolde's hand in marriage, he wins
her by killing a local dragon, though a false steward interposes a rival
claim to the deed. At this point, Isolde discovers that Tantris is the
Tristan who killed her uncle, and only just resists the impulse to
assassinate him in his bath. A striking emotional reversal occurs when
on the return trip to Cornwall, Tristan and Isolde mistakenly drink a
love potion that had been supplied for Isolde and Mark. In Eilhart,
the potion is so strong that the lovers cannot be separated for so much
as a day without dying, but, as in Béroul, it wears off after four years.
Deception, suspense, and anguish characterize the further adventures of
the lovers and Isolde's faithful companion Brangaine, as they attempt
to hide their irresistible passion from Mark. A period of banishment
during which the lovers wander in the forest tests the strength of their
attachment, but eventually Isolde must return to Mark. Tristan, separated
from Isolde the Fair, marries the Breton princess Isolde of the White
Hands, but cannot bring himself to consummate the marriage. Dying
once again from an envenomed wound, he sends for Isolde the Fair.
As in the Theseus myth, the ship bringing her carries white sails to
mark her arrival, but Isolde of Brittany tells Tristan they are black.
When Isolde the Fair appears at his bedside, Tristan has already
succumbed, and she dies on his body.

While all the verse romances of Tristan have important positive traits,
Gottfried von Strassburg's treatment of this material is particulary
effective. Critics have expressed concern over Gottfried's evocation of
courtly love as a rival religion, with its own chapel in a forest cave
where the lovers are united; his questioning of established Christianity
and the social order is made apparent by their effect on the lovers. Its
unusual intellectual perspective and elegance of style contribute to
deepening the poem's interest.[25]

Two thirteenth-century prose Tristan romances in French attach the
story to the Arthurian world.[26] New chivalric adventures are given to
Tristram, who strives to become a knight of the Round Table. He
loses some of his individual character as the hunter and harper becomes
one of many Arthurian knights-errant. In the process King Mark

deteriorates still more drastically, as epic degeneration takes hold on his character. Often a reasonable or even appealing figure in the verse romances of Tristan, Mark becomes the epitome of cowardice and treachery, the ultimate antichivalric king. It is he who kills Tristan, stabbing him in the back, in the prose romances. In the long run, proximity to Arthur would not prove healthy for Tristan and his legend.

The Perceval romances. The unfinished condition of Chrétien's *Perceval* and the inherent fascination of the grail narrative naturally led later authors to attempt the subject in a variety of continuations. The most successful of these are, in prose, the French *Perlesvaus* and, in verse, Wolfram von Eschenbach's *Parzifal;* the Welsh romance of *Peredur* and the *Didot Perceval* should also be mentioned.

Perlesvaus, dated around 1191–1212, begins after its hero Perlesvaus (a variant of Perceval), has failed to ask the all-important question that would heal his host, the Fisher King. As a result, Britain becomes barren. Arthur undertakes a pilgrimage to Glastonbury to discover the cause of his own and the kingdom's malaise, whereupon Gawain, Lancelot, and Perlesvaus proceed on successive grail quests. Lancelot is treated much more sympathetically than in the *Quest of the Holy Grail;* Arthur and Guinevere are given a son, Loholt (from the Welsh Lachau), who is killed by Kay. Combat against Kay, Brian of the Isles, and other rebels, Arthur's final vision of the grail, and Perlesvaus's departure to a mystical island Other World end this quite individual version of Arthurian history. Special interest has been directed to the *Perlesvaus*'s interest in warfare for the defense of the faith, and to its effective prose style, but in general this interesting work has not received the critical notice it deserves.[27]

A quite different fate has overtaken Wolfram von Eschenbach's *Parzifal.*[28] After a period of obscurity from the sixteenth to the nineteenth century, modern critical acclaim has established it as the greatest German epic. Wolfram von Eschenbach describes himself as an impoverished knight, and, less plausibly, as illiterate. Hotly engaged in the literary combats of his day, he may simply be distancing himself from contemporaries who boast of their own learning. His *Parzifal,* begun around 1200–1210, acknowledges Chrétien's *Perceval* as a major source, but in style and content it has been recognized as an exceedingly inventive work. Wolfram's grail is a stone, not a dish; it sustains and protects those around it, notably its divinely chosen keepers, the grail family, and the celibate order of knights who serve it. The crusading adventures of Parzifal's father Gahmuret are followed by the familiar story of the

young and naïf Parzifal. Wolfram interlaces Parzifal's furious search for
the grail castle, the scene of his failure, with Gawain's courtly exploits.
Here Parzifal's steadfast adoration of his wife Cundwiramurs is played
against Gawain's adept pursuit of courtly love *(minne)*.[29] Parzifal's
passage through a period of questioning God leads him to a new
spiritual awareness that prepares him to become the grail king. Distinctive
to Wolfram von Eschenbach are his deliberately rough and complex
style, his fondness for unpronounceable names, and his unusually positive
characterizations of heathens like Parzifal's Saracen half-brother Fierefiz.
Wolfram's contemporary Gottfried von Strassburg records his disgust
with Wolfram's wild imagination and obscure writing, but the seventy
surviving manuscripts of *Parzifal* tell us that in medieval Germany
Wolfram's work enjoyed the popularity it has regained today.

The Gawain romances. The Arthurian chronicle tradition discussed in the first chapter demonstrated Gawain's early prominence as
a key Arthurian warrior. A third group of romances can be collected
from the mass of medieval European Arthurian narratives. These works
center around Arthur's nephew Gawain. Chrétien's *Yvain, Lancelot,* and
Perceval, like Wolfram's *Parzifal,* use the established hero Gawain as
a standard against whom to measure their principal Arthurian heroes.
Certain French prose romances continue the process, denigrating Gawain
to the advantage of others. The *Quest of the Holy Grail* and the prose
Tristan offer a particularly sour view of Gawain's traditional courtesy
as, basically, promiscuity. In these works, he is fickle, self-centered, and
vengeful. In French verse romances like *Le Chevalier à l'epée (The
Knight of the Sword), La Mule sans frein (The Unbridled Mule), L'Atre
perilleux (The Perilous Graveyard), Meriadeuc, Hunbaut,* or *La Vengeance
Radiguel (Vengeance for Radiguel),* Gawain emerges triumphant from
a series of often comic or even slapstick adventures. More positive
handling of Gawain can also be seen in the German *Diu krône (The
Crown)* of Heinrich von dem Türlin, Gawain's own grail romance, and
in the Middle Dutch romances.[30] He remains a crucial figure in the
Middle English romance as well.

Almost no European literature is without its Arthurian romances.
They exist in Old Norse, Hebrew, Yiddish, Greek, and of course Spanish
and Catalan, Portuguese, Provençal, Italian, and Serbo-Croatian.[31] From
the twelfth to the sixteenth century, Arthur and his court retained their
fascination for authors and readers far removed from Britain or the
fifth century. It is fair to say, though, that the heyday of Arthurian
romance on the Continent was the thirteenth century: by the later

1360s, when the poet and historian Jean Froissart took up the subject of the young King Arthur's court in his long verse romance *Méliador,* his French contemporaries had deserted the field for some time.[32]

The English Romances

In England, the Arthurian romance tradition proved a somewhat different matter. To begin with, English authors derived much of their material by translating from French sources, just as their counterparts were doing across Europe. Nevertheless, native English characteristics have been detected by many scholars. The English verse romances largely ignore the epic degeneration of both Arthur and Gawain in the French prose narratives, possibly out of patriotic support for these time-honored Britons. The wilder side of courtly love is a less popular feature of the English Arthurian scene: properly married young heroes seem to be more appealing to medieval English readers. The quest of the Holy Grail apparently never caught on in Middle English: Sir Thomas Malory is the only medieval English author to include it; in England this religious facet of the Arthurian legend only found appreciation in the nineteenth century.

The most influential Arthurian work of the English Middle Ages, Malory's mid-fifteenth-century *Morte Darthur,* is treated in the next chapter. This section focuses on the English Arthurian romances up to Malory, with special attention devoted to a work that may in fact be the masterpiece of the English Arthurian tradition, the fourteenth-century alliterative romance *Sir Gawain and the Green Knight.*

English Arthurian romances. The twenty-seven known English Arthurian romances vary widely in quality and content. Omitting for the moment Malory's *Morte Darthur* and *Sir Gawain and the Green Knight,* the heterogeneous collection of English works remaining contains some impressive items, as well as some regrettable failures. In date, they range from the thirteenth to the sixteenth centuries, and their techniques include the ballad, prose, alliterative verse, minstrel tail-rhyme stanzas, and Geoffrey Chaucer's mature decasyllabic couplets. Generally most of the English romances seem shorter than their French predecessors, and the English poets seem for the most part free from the cyclic compulsion that overtook many of the French authors. Many narratives seem to have been composed for popular rather than courtly audiences, though this is always a hazardous determination to make. Further contrasts in audience and book production are apparent when

the surviving English manuscripts, few of which are illuminated, are
set against more sumptuous Continental display manuscripts.[33]

A number of sixteenth-century ballads preserve Arthurian themes, for
example "King Arthur and King Cornwall" and the incomplete "Marriage of Sir Gawain" in the Percy Folio MS. "The Boy and the Mantle,"
praised by George Lyman Kittredge, uses an enchanted mantle to test
the chastity of the ladies of Arthur's court; the only successful knight
is Craddocke (in the ballad's French sources, Caradoc Briebras). These
works record perhaps the last gasp of medieval Arthurian composition,
representing later reworkings of material presented earlier in the form
of romances.[34]

The surviving romances themselves vary in quality from Henry
Lovelich's plodding translations from the French, the *Holy Grail* and
Merlin of ca. 1460, to the high art of Chaucer's "Wife of Bath's
Tale." Among the more successful efforts in this direction should be
cited *Arthour and Merlin,* written around 1250–1300, and preserved
in the Auchinleck MS., now in the Advocates Library, Edinburgh. This
is probably the most famous English romance anthology, and may have
been owned at one time by Chaucer.[35] *Arthour and Merlin* is a competent
abridged version of Arthurian history from before Arthur's birth through
his coronation and early exploits against the recalcitrant British kings.
The poet makes interesting use of interpolated lyrics.[36] *Ywain and
Gawain* (ca. 1350) is the only surviving Middle English translation of
any romance of Chrétien de Troyes. Its poet condenses *Yvain* to produce
a colloquial, direct, and essentially unreflective adventure story (British
Library MS. Cotton Galba E.ix.).[37]

Gawain was evidently a favorite character in English romances, where
he is treated much more respectfully than in French prose narratives.
He appears in the majority of the extant English Arthurian works, and
is frequently the protagonist. Thomas Chestre's *Libeaus desconus (The
Fair Unknown),* whose popularity is attested by its six surviving copies,
retells the story of Gawain's son Ginglain and his disenchantment of
a lamia by means of a kiss (the *fier baiser* motif) in the ruined Roman
city of Sinadoine (Segontium). Gawain himself responds in kind to the
slapstick challenge of the *Carl of Carlisle* (1400). He also figures in
The Awntyrs off Arthure at the Tarne Wathelyne, which survives in late
fourteenth- and fifteenth-century manuscripts. Properly the adventures
are those of Gawain and Guinevere, who receive a lecture from the
ghost of Guinevere's mother on the evils of courtly life; in the second
half of the romance, Gawain participates in a judicial duel against the

Scot Galeron. In *The Avowing of King Arthur* of around 1425, Gawain joins Arthur, Kay, and Baldwin of Britain in performing individual chivalric vows. Here, though, the honors are captured by Baldwin, whose vow is a sceptical philosophy of life rather than a knight-errant's vaunt. The *Avowing of Arthur* is notable for its portrayal of Arthur as an active knight, a humorist, and good companion. It ranks among the best of the stanzaic tail-rhyme romances. *The Gest of Gawain* (ca. 1450) continues the tradition of Gawain the seducer.[38]

The most popular of the narratives associated with Gawain seems to have been the story represented in *The Wedding of Sir Gawen and Dame Ragnell* (ca. 1450), and in the ballad of *The Marriage of Sir Gawain* in the Percy Folio MS.[39] Geoffrey Chaucer's Wife of Bath tells the same story in the *Canterbury Tales* as an Arthurian story without naming Gawain as its hero. John Gower's *Tale of Florent* and the ballads of *King Henry* and *The Knight and the Shepherd's Daughter* bear witness to the story's vigorous independent existence outside Arthurian romance. *The Wedding of Sir Gawain,* identified by at least one critic (P. J. C. Field) as an early work of Sir Thomas Malory, presents an Arthur threatened with execution by the sinister Gromer Somyr Joure; to escape, the king must find out what women most desire. A truly repulsive old hag demands Gawain's hand in marriage as a reward for telling Arthur the answer. On the wedding night, Gawain is invited to choose whether he would prefer his wife to be beautiful by day and ugly by night or the converse. By surrendering the choice to her, with a kiss, Gawain frees Ragnell from her stepmother's spell, and restores her beauty permanently. With minor variations, this is the pattern also followed in the "Marriage of Gawain."

The "Wife of Bath's Tale" of around 1390 alters the story, no doubt due to variant sources and Geoffrey Chaucer's own interests as a writer.[40] The Wife of Bath tells her tale to enforce her radical point of view—that the wife should have sovereignty in marriage. Her knight is young and unnamed; in the first lines of the tale he is sentenced to die for rape and then reprieved for a year by Arthur's queen. Presiding over a court of ladies that has reminded some critics of the courts of love first associated with Eleanor of Aquitaine and her daughter Marie of Champagne, Chaucer's queen sends the knight out to discover womens' greatest desire. From the start, Chaucer plays up the fairy-tale distance of the "days of King Arthur," and the mysterious appearance of the ancient hag by the forest side, set against the human chagrin of the rapist knight forced into an unwanted marriage. Chaucer's old hag

responds to his disgust with an extended wedding-night lecture on the
merits of poverty and ugliness, and on the nature of innate nobility,
"gentilesse," which comes from noble deeds, not birth. Her offer to
the knight is also significantly changed; he must decide whether he
wants an ugly, faithful wife, or a beautiful one of dubious morality.
Offering her the decision shows that he has learned from his quest,
and ensures that she will be both beautiful and true.

Other brief references in Chaucer's "Squire's Tale" and "Nun's Priest's
Tale" demonstrate the poet's awareness of the Arthurian romances and
their English audience: the prose *Lancelot* was particularly admired by
women, according to the Nun's Priest. In the "Wife of Bath's Tale"
Arthur provides a magical setting for the narrative, more than anything
else. Still, the poem itself ranks among the most successful English
Arthurian pieces, for its apt characterizations, its tightened plot structure
and effective comic reversals, and naturally as an outstanding example
of Chaucer's mature style as a narrative poet. By belatedly giving this
tale to the Wife of Bath in place of her original *fabliau,* the bawdier
"Shipman's Tale," Chaucer stresses the Wife's imagination, enriching
an already vivid portrait. The Wife of Bath, a self-proclaimed authority
on the desires of her sex, can enter wholeheartedly into the central
question of the narrative: her interest in the Arthurian world carries her
beyond the antifeminist stereotypes on which she stands into an irresistible
fantasy.

The late fourteenth-century stanzaic *Morte Arthur* of B.L. MS. Harley
2252 (ff. 86–133) is still neglected by criticism, though its recognition
as an important source for the final books of Malory's *Morte Darthur*
has drawn more attention to it in recent years.[41] This romance draws
on the French *Mort Artu* for its compact, dramatic account of the last
days of King Arthur. It begins with Arthur calling a tournament in
response to Gaynor's interesting complaint that the honor of the Round
Table is fading. An astute selection of events follows. Lancelot's encounter
with the Fair Maid of Ascolat leads to a breach with Gaynor. Gaynor
is unjustly accused of poisoning a knight at her banquet and defended
by the always magnanimous Lancelot. The lovers are betrayed to Arthur
by Agravain and Mordred. Lancelot's rescue of Gaynor from the stake,
with his accidental killing of Gawayn's brothers, Gaheriet and Gaheris,
leads Arthur and Gawayn to attack, carrying their warfare into Lancelot's
own territories in France. Arthur is called back to deal with Mordred's
rebellion. Gawayn is killed, and the king carried off by ship to Avalon;

Arthur's tomb appears at Glastonbury the next day. After a last poignant meeting, Lancelot and Gaynor both die in religious orders.

Among the distinctive touches of the stanzaic *Morte Arthur* should be included the fateful moment before the last battle on Salisbury Plain, when a knight drawing his sword to kill an adder unintentionally breaks the truce between Arthur and Mordred. Malory owes to the stanzaic *Morte Arthur* an important share of the drama of the closing books of his work. The final interview between Lancelot and Guinevere in her convent at Aymesbury may have originated here, or in an idiosyncratic French manuscript. Certainly the close verbal similarities between Malory's great renunciation scene and that in the stanzaic *Morte Arthur* demonstrate its contribution unequivocally. The verse is workmanlike: an acute sense of character and action allow the poet to focus in on the essential elements of fate and personality that combine to create Arthur's tragedy.

While the stanzaic *Morte Arthur* is grounded in the Vulgate Cycle, the alliterative *Morte Arthure* derives its considerable effects from the chronicle tradition of Arthur's conquests.[42] Malory's heavy dependence on the alliterative *Morte Arthure* in the Winchester MS. account of Arthur's Roman wars has brought the alliterative *Morte* to the center of critical controversy in this century. Its use of traditional English alliterative principles of versification connects it with the fourteenth-century alliterative revival, a poetic movement to which belong masterworks like William Langland's *Piers Plowman* and the anonymous *Sir Gawain and the Green Knight*. The alliterative *Morte Arthure* deserves to be ranked highly even among this illustrious company.[43] The single surviving copy appears in Robert Thornton's MS. anthology of romances, Lincoln Cathedral Library MS. 91 of about 1440; the romance itself has been dated around 1400. The alliterative poet's main source is Geoffrey of Monmouth's biography of Arthur as retold in Wace and Layamon. Reminiscences of Charlemagne and Alexander romances, readings in non-Arthurian Middle English literature, and even references to contemporary historical events have been noted in the alliterative *Morte Arthure*.

The romance takes up the story of Arthur with the banquet celebrating Arthur's conquests, rudely interrupted by ambassadors from Rome demanding his submission to the emperor Lucius. Arthur and his knights respond defiantly with vows to perform military exploits against the Romans in France. This event almost certainly derives from the late thirteenth-century Alexander romance, the *Voeux du paon (Vows of the Peacock);* this type of chivalric vow also became popular in real life,

finding imitators at the courts of Edward I, Edward III, and Duke
Philip the Good of Burgundy.[44] Arthur's voyage to France is punctuated
by a disturbing nightmare of a dragon fighting a bear. This Arthur's
wise men interpret as a presage of victory. The alliterative *Morte Arthure*
offers a vivid description of Arthur's single combat with the giant of
Mont-Saint-Michel. The defeat of Lucius, Gawain's conversion of a
pagan opponent, and a new foray into Italy are followed by Mordred's
revolt and Arthur's last battle. There is no nonsense here about Avalon
or Arthur's potential return; the king's body is carried to Glastonbury
and buried there with impressive simplicity.

The alliterative *Morte Arthure*'s Arthur should perhaps be seen among
the strongest images of the king as a central figure on his own romance.
The poet makes good use of Arthur's prophetic dreams; a second vision
of the wheel of fortune shows Arthur the other eight Worthies as
warnings of his destined end. Critics have commented on the Nine
Worthies motif as a link between the alliterative *Parlement of the Three
Ages, Sir Gawain and the Green Knight,* and the alliterative *Morte
Arthure.*[45] Here this traditional group of great chivalric heroes may be
linked with the poem's concerns about kingship, fortune, and the savagery
of battle. Mordred and Arthur both lament Gawain in moving terms,
yet despite this common loss, they still must destroy one another. In
its descriptive artistry, epic action, and narrative balance, the alliterative
Morte Arthure stands well to the fore of the English Arthurian romances.

Sir Gawain and the Green Knight.   The greatest acclaim among
English verse romances has been bestowed on the later fourteenth-century
alliterative poem *Sir Gawain and the Green Knight.* B.L. MS. Cotton
Nero A.x. contains the one surviving copy of the poem, as well as the
alliterative religious poems *Pearl, Patience,* and *Cleanness.* Resemblances
of dialect and technique have led many scholars to postulate that all
four of these exceptional poems were written by the same author. The
dialect of *Sir Gawain* has been localized specifically within a limited
area of southeast Cheshire or northeast Staffordshire. Nevertheless, in
spite of much ingenious detective work, no author has yet been identified.
The manuscript itself seems to be the copy of a more expensive volume;
its rough illuminations portray a number of scenes from the poem. Its
composition has been dated at roughly 1370–90.[46]

In terms of basic literary technique, *Sir Gawain and the Green Knight*
belongs, like the alliterative *Morte Arthure,* to the alliterative revival of
the fourteenth century. The poet uses the long Middle English alliterative
line in 101 stanzas of varying length; a short rhymed "bob and wheel"

of five lines follows the main stanza. The mathematical planning of *Sir Gawain* has excited the curiosity of more than one theorist. The poet's interest in the five points of the pentangle on Gawain's shield and the five groups of five virtues they represent has also encouraged speculation in this direction.[47]

Sir Gawain opens with an epic reminiscence of Britain's legendary Trojan origins. The narrator then focuses in on Arthur's court in the midst of a lavish Christmas feast. Detailed description is a strong point in *Sir Gawain,* as it was in the alliterative *Morte Arthure.* The *Gawain* poet's Arthur is young, boyish, and active. Following the precedent established in the French cycle romances, Arthur refuses to eat until some marvel or adventure presents itself before the assembled company. His vigil is interrupted by the appearance of a gigantic green knight, who rides into the hall on his green horse to propose a "Christmas game." He invites one of Arthur's knights to chop off his head: in a year the Green Knight will conclude the "beheading game" by administering a blow to Arthur's champion. Arthur himself takes up the challenge, only to be hastily replaced by his nephew Gawain. In one of the more horrific effects of the narrative, Gawain beheads the Green Knight, who calmly picks up his head, directs Gawain to seek him in a year at the Green Chapel, and rides off.

A year passes; as winter approaches, Gawain prepares to journey in search of the Green Chapel. The poet discusses Gawain's arming and armor at some length, particularly his shield with its five-pointed star, the "pentangle" or "endless knot," representing Gawain's many virtues, and its image of the Virgin Mary. So armed, Gawain sets off into the wilderness, through a disagreeably bleak landscape. Just on the verge of the holiday season, he arrives at a castle where he is welcomed by its affable lord, his attractive wife, and a mysterious old lady. Gawain learns that the Green Chapel is nearby, and agrees to spend the intervening days before his appointment resting at the castle. As a form of amusement, his host proposes a new "Christmas game." He will ride out to hunt while Gawain remains indoors. At the end of the day, the two men will exchange their winnings.

This "exchange of winnings" agreement leads the poem into a series of parallel events. Each day, the lord of the castle rides out to hunt deer, a boar, and finally a fox. Meanwhile back at the castle, Gawain is confronted by the lady, who slips into his bedchamber, she says, to receive lessons in courtly love from the most famous lover of King Arthur's court. Here the poet plays on Gawain's formidable reputation in the French romances for sexual prowess. All the same, this Gawain evades the lady's temptations with exquisite diplomacy, and proffers to her husband the kisses he has won during the day, naturally without revealing their source. Only on the third day does Gawain conceal the lady's gift of a green scarf—a magic talisman, she tells him, that can preserve his life.

The final division of *Sir Gawain* depicts Gawain's journey to the Green Chapel. He rejects his guide's helpful suggestion that he back out at the last minute, and proceeds to the uncanny cleft in the rocks to which he is directed. When the Green Knight appears, he feints at Gawain and then gives him a slight neck wound. This, Gawain discovers, is his punishment for breaking his agreement and hiding the green scarf. Gawain's failure in "lewte" was occasioned, the Green Knight says, by a very natural emotion, "For you loved your life." The Green Knight, it turns out, was also Gawain's host Bertilak de Hautdesert. His supernatural transformation was produced by Arthur's half-sister Morgan le Fay, the old lady of the castle, to terrify Guinevere. The lady's seductive visits to Gawain's bedroom were made at her husband's request. In spite of the Green Knight's affability, Gawain reproaches himself for cowardice, covetousness, and susceptibility to the female sex's traditional treachery. He vows to wear the green scarf forever as a badge of shame. On returning to court, Gawain confesses his failure publicly. The members of Arthur's court adopt the green sash themselves as a mark of fellowship with Gawain. The romance ends, much as it began, with their laughter.

The nature of Gawain's fault and its testing is still a matter of debate among scholars. Some read the romance pessimistically, in the light of the religious poems of MS. Cotton Nero A.x. This school of thought sees *Sir Gawain* as an indictment of the secular chivalry represented by Arthur's court. For many others, Gawain's reliance on the green sash is a lapse of Christian faith in the Virgin Mary, so that his primary failure of loyalty is religious. Other readers focus on the impossible virtues represented by the pentangle shield; the test restores a cocky Gawain to humility. *Sir Gawain*'s thoughtful investigation certainly tests the human capacity to achieve perfection. If Gawain falls short, it is because he is a human being, like his comrades of the Round Table. Whether this is a positive or negative conclusion depends ultimately on the temperament of the reader.[48]

Sir Gawain and the Green Knight apparently derives its plot from a variety of sources; no one precursor has yet been identified that combines all the key events of the romance. The "Beheading Game" figures in Irish legend. "Bricriu's Feast" (the *Fled Bricrend*) involves the hero Cuchullain in such a contest. French Gawain romances like *La Mule sans frein* reproduce this element. Parallels for the seductive lady can also be found elsewhere, within and beyond the limits of the romance. Other elements in the story seem epic in origin, the opening and Gawain's arming scene, for instance. Arthurian boarhunts occur frequently in Celtic literature. Morgan's magic, enmity, and provision of dangerous tests for Arthur's knights can be traced back to the French Arthurian romances of the thirteenth century. The greenness of the Green Knight and his hunting have suggested to some investigators that a vegetation myth lies behind the narrative. Interest has also been generated by the manuscript notation "Honi soit qui mal y pense" (Shamed be he who thinks evil of it), the motto of Edward III's Order of the Garter, and by the suggestion that the green sash might correspond in some way to the garter worn by Edward's chosen band of knights.[49]

Whatever their disparate theories of its origin or meaning, twentieth-century readers generally think well of *Sir Gawain and the Green Knight*. While its dialect and complex alliteration make the original difficult of access to the nonspecialist, in translation *Sir Gawain* may be the most immediately appealing of all English romances. Its brilliantly worked descriptive surface, psychological intuition, and the combat of wits it presents irresistibly engage the reader's attention. The questions of loyalty and courage are explored, not to an absolute conclusion, but through one circuit of the endless knot. The whole poem stresses the idea of play, of a "Christmas game," and through that game conveys its message with a deft hand.

Conclusion. Because any number of new adventures can always be woven into the plot, the romance's open-ended plot structure has misled too many authors into creating monsters of interminable length. This chapter must fight the same impulse to mention and describe just one more narrative. Enough has been said, perhaps, to establish at least the infinite variety of the medieval Arthurian romance, if not to catalogue every deserving instance of it.

Chapter Three

Sir Thomas Malory's
Morte Darthur

With Sir Thomas Malory, the Arthurian legend in English reaches a new phase. Geoffrey of Monmouth set down a complete history of Arthur, as far as we know for the first time, in the early twelfth century. The French romance writers of the later twelfth and thirteenth centuries translated the Celtic legends into a new fictional form. Then, sometime in the mid–fifteenth century, possibly while in prison, an English knight named Sir Thomas Malory wrote what became the most influential Arthurian work in English. His narrative of King Arthur's life and his knights' adventures has retained its grip on succeeding generations of authors and readers up to the present. Nothing that came after it seems to have escaped its touch. The Arthurian writings of Alfred, Lord Tennyson, T. H. White, John Steinbeck, Mary Stewart, and Marion Zimmer Bradley all testify in their own ways to its power.

One reason why Malory's *Morte Darthur* has maintained its ascendency over the years is, of course, the fact that it is a masterpiece of English prose, one of the first great prose compositions in the language. No modernized edition or paraphrase has ever been able to reproduce the impact of Malory's style at its best; the attempts range from the respectable to the atrocious. Never before in English had the history of the Round Table been retold so impressively.

This brief chapter can hardly resolve the many ongoing debates over Malory's life and work. Its first concern must be to describe the *Morte Darthur* itself, and its main objective to locate Malory within the whole sweep of Arthurian literature. By focusing on the links that tie the *Morte Darthur* to its medieval predecessors, and charting its later influence, we can plot the vital role that Malory's work has played in English and American Arthuriana. Understanding Malory's distinctive approach to his subject unquestionably helps in the assessment of his ultimate impact on his successors.

Sir Thomas Malory: The Issue of Identity

The identity of the Sir Thomas Malory who wrote the *Morte Darthur* has been a matter of critical debate since the late William Matthews entered the lists in 1966 with *The Ill-Framed Knight*.[1] Up to that point, Kittredge's identification of the author of the *Morte Darthur* as Sir Thomas Malory of Newbold Revel in Warwickshire (c. 1400–71) had been accepted by most scholars, with some reservations. This knight's lively career included service in France and northern England under Richard Beauchamp, earl of Warwick, but also imprisonment on charges of cattle rustling, rape, armed robbery of a monastery, and several dramatic escapes.[2]

Modern scholars disconcerted by this alarming record have reacted variously to the jarring contrast between the chivalric idealism of the *Morte Darthur* and the biography of its apparent author. Some have defended Kittredge's Malory by pointing out the problems of late medieval legal language and the absence of any surviving trial documents. "Rape" in particular had a number of meanings in the fifteenth-century courtroom, ranging from the modern sense of the word to abduction.[3] A second line of defense is to censure the whole fifteenth century as an age of violence, political and moral decline, and sheer escapism. Malory would then be merely a man of his times. But this image of the later Middle Ages, popularized by the glorious prose of Johan Huizinga's *Waning of the Middle Ages,* is now regarded by most historians as a caricature.[4]

A third strategy for rescuing the *Morte Darthur* has been to search the records for a more respectable Sir Thomas Malory. In *The Ill-Framed Knight* Matthews offered three additional candidates as potential authors of the *Morte Darthur*. Of these, he preferred a Thomas Malory of Studley and Hutton in Yorkshire, who was born in the 1420s or '30s and still living in 1471.[5] R. Griffith in *Aspects of Malory* advocates Thomas Malory of Papworth Saint Agnes on the Cambridge-Huntingdonshire border.[6]

The *Morte Darthur* itself offers little clear evidence of its writer's biography. Malory describes himself as a "knyght presoner" and repeatedly asks his readers to pray for his "good delyveraunce."[7] He dates the final section of his work as ended "in the ninth yere of the reygne of Kyng Edward the Fourth"—that is, 1469–70 (Vinaver, 726). Kittredge's Malory of Newbold Revel was unquestionably both a knight and in prison on more than one occasion. Matthews's and Griffith's Malories may or may not have been: evidence of their fulfillment of these two necessary conditions is less secure. Matthews cites linguistic evidence of northern dialect forms, and Malory's use of the Middle English alliterative *Morte Arthure* as a source. Alliterative poetry was little appreciated in southern England in the later Middle Ages, as Chaucer and William Caxton, Malory's printer, both bear witness.[8] On Griffith's side is a possible connection between the Papworth Saint Agnes Malory and Anthony Woodville, Earl Rivers, which would link him both with the remnants of the duke of Bedford's excellent library and with Woodville's publisher, William Caxton, whose edition of the *Morte Darthur* appeared in 1485. Hilton Kelliher has discussed further points of contact between Woodville and the Malory Manuscript, now in the British Library, which remains one of only three surviving sources for Malory's text.[9]

Of these, the Winchester or Malory MS. was discovered in 1934 by W. F. Oakeshott in the library of Winchester College. It is the only known manuscript of the *Morte Darthur*. Lotte Hellinga has shown that Caxton knew it; indeed, he had it in his printing workship at Westminster around 1481, where some careless person left wet pages of printed matter on top of it.[10] Whether or not Caxton had any additional manuscript source is, again, still a matter of debate. His printed edition of Malory contains many adjustments that might have been made either by the author himself or by an energetic publisher. Eugène Vinaver, James Spisak, and William Matthews have all been inclined to think that these changes may have been Malory's own, though Hellinga questions this assumption.[11] A substantial number of scholars still prefer Caxton's 1485 printed version of the *Morte Darthur* to that of the manuscript for this reason. Two copies of Caxton's volume, representing slightly different states of his text, are preserved in the John Rylands Library, Manchester, and the Pierpont Morgan Library in New York.

It would naturally delight most critics and readers of Malory to be able to answer the question of who Malory really was. It seems clear, however, that the present historical and literary evidence cannot provide an unassailable solution. Further research may yet establish one of the candidates already discussed as the dominant Arthurian writer in English. At this moment the debate on authorship mostly involves philosophical issues. Is it necessary for a great author to be a virtuous human being? Must the writer who recommends a system of morality to us also live by his precepts? These problems led scholars to question Kittredge's identification of Malory in the first place. Whether they should have done so is a debatable issue in its own right. Fortunately, it is not necessary to resolve any one of these complex quarrels in order to appreciate the magnificence of the *Morte Darthur*. That, at least, stands on its own.

Malory and His Sources

When Sir Thomas Malory's work is seen in relation to the whole body of English and American Arthurian literature up to the present, the *Morte Darthur*'s importance as a source is clear. It is true that from the late sixteenth to the nineteenth centuries the handful of authors who attempted Arthurian compositions neglected the *Morte Darthur,* usually in favor of Geoffrey of Monmouth, apparently a more historical source, or in favor of their own embellishments, like Dryden's Oswald and Emmeline.[12] But with the rediscovery of the *Morte Darthur* in the nineteenth century, Malory's volume reasserted its position as the standard Arthurian narrative in English. The vast majority of English and American Arthurian works since then have founded their views of the legend on Malory as the definitive history of Arthur, though they may not all admit as much. A reading of Malory is, therefore, fundamental to understanding all that comes after him.

Looking backward to assign Malory a place among medieval Arthurian writers changes our perspective radically. For the student of the Middle Ages, Malory can hardly pose as a precursor, the primitive original from which later narratives derive their basic facts and characters. That position, if it belongs to any one writer, is Geoffrey of Monmouth's. If there is any primary "history" of Arthur, it is Geoffrey's account of him in the *Historia regum Britanniae*. Malory's work arrived at the close of the Middle Ages. It postdates all the chief medieval Arthurian writings, and, indeed, makes use of a wide variety of them. Malory's greatness properly lies in his genius as an adapter, and as a writer of enduring English prose. Only rarely does he add episodes that are completely his own, though when he does they are often surprising. For the most part, it is his ability to select key events from the unwieldy mass of Arthurian mythology available to him in French and English, and to retell them masterfully, that marks him as an artist. Where Geoffrey of Monmouth forged fictional history from oral recollections and classical reminiscences, for the most part Malory was content to revisualize and focus the tales invented by his predecessors.

Malory's contemporary and publisher, William Caxton, summed up the state of Arthurian literature in the fifteenth century when he remarked that so many books about Arthur had been written by then that it was "a world / or a thyng incredyble to byleue."[13] Some students of Malory have indeed attempted to establish his identity by locating the library that the "knight prisoner" pillaged for his multiple sources. Current views suggest that it must have been a substantial collection, perhaps equal to those of the dukes of Burgundy or Bedford.[14] No one French or English volume has yet been found that gives all of Malory's source material in compact form. Some sections of the *Morte Darthur* appear to be more or less original inventions of Malory's—at least, no definite prototype for them has yet been established. In other places Malory relies so closely on identifiable sources that it is clear he must have had the book in front of him as he wrote; no one's memory for a prose text, or even for alliterative or stanzaic poetry, was that good, within or beyond the Middle Ages. Malory's account of King Arthur's Roman wars in the Malory MS. follows on the heels of the alliterative *Morte Arthure* so closely that it preserves much of the poem's alliteration.[15] The remaining narrative wanders in and out of direct translation from the French. The thirteenth-century prose cycles provided Malory with other important sources, notably the *Suite du Merlin,* the French prose *Tristan* and the prose *Lancelot,* incorporating accounts of the quest of the Holy Grail and the last days of King Arthur. The late-fourteenth-century English stanzaic *Morte Arthur* gave Malory a useful alternative version of these final events.[16] All this certainly suggests that Malory had a first-rate library at his disposal. A fair number of scholars have observed that this is an uncommon situation for a prisoner, as we imagine medieval prisons.[17]

Another source for Malory's picture of Arthur's world was historical. Echoes of a wide range of political and military events of the fifteenth century have been detected in the *Morte Darthur.* Its Arthurian geography includes references to French place-names that suggest Malory was familiar with Aquitaine. The English campaigns there in 1453 could have provided him with this specialized knowledge.[18] Arthur's French invasion to battle the Romans mirrors that of Henry V, a patriotic military reminiscence that few Englishmen of the later fifteenth century could have resisted.[19] Elsewhere in the *Morte Darthur,* Malory seems to betray some Lancastrian sympathies. His comment on the political fickleness of the English seems particularly apt, coming from an observer of the Wars of the Roses.[20]

The Narrative Plan of the *Morte Darthur*

Of course, Malory did more than simply record the words of his sources to make his own highly individual volume, though there are long stretches of the *Morte Darthur* that can only be classified as brilliant straight translations. His narrative organization should itself be seen as an important original contribution to the Arthurian legend. But while Malory's narrative may have been read and applauded by many generations, the nature of that narrative has been the subject of lively debates since the time of its first publication.[21] What kind of a book about King Arthur did Malory devise? Scholarly responses to this question have been diverse in the extreme. Early historians of the novel hailed the *Morte Darthur* as "the first English novel," which it certainly is not.[22] Other critics have preferred to identify the *Morte Darthur* as a prose epic, or, perhaps, as an attempt at a vernacular history of Arthur, innocent of any fictional intent.[23] Eugène Vinaver, one of the most eminent scholars to write on Malory in this century, regards the *Morte Darthur* as "a series of self-contained stories" or separate romances rather than a single unified work.[24] Nevertheless, many readers still see the *Morte Darthur* as a connected prose romance, if an unprecedented one. Malory seems to have replaced the interlace pattern of episodes that tied together the French cycle romances he used as sources with a more linear arrangement of events, narrowing the action to concentrate on a smaller number of major characters.[25]

As many critics read it now, Malory's book appears to have three main divisions. It begins and ends with the biography of Arthur, as narrated in chronicle and romance from Geoffrey of Monmouth and the *Suite du Merlin* on. The first event of the volume is the initial meeting of Arthur's parents, Uther Pendragon, the beleaguered king of England, and Duchess Igraine of Cornwall, the loyal wife of another man. It ends with the death of Arthur's principal knight, Sir Lancelot of the Lake, and the departure of the remaining knights of the Round Table to fight in the Holy Land.

The earliest third of Malory's account concerns the rise of Arthur to the kingship of Britain. It shows Arthur pulling the sword from the stone to establish his right to the throne, and describes his defeat of the rival British kings, and of the Roman Lucius in France. This first section also tells of the founding of the Round Table, and introduces many of its principal knights—Kay, Gawain, Lancelot, and Gareth, among others—as well as Arthur's chief advisor, Merlin the enchanter, Arthur's bride Guinevere, and his half-sister Morgan le Fay and Morgause. Malory prepares his readers early for Arthur's last battle by presenting Arthur's incestuous affair with Morgause, and the birth of their son Mordred.

The second third of the book, "The Book of Sir Tristram of Lyonesse," depicts the Round Table at its height. Here the great love triangle of Tristram, Isolde, and King Mark of Cornwall is introduced, paralleling the much more complex relationship of Lancelot, Guinevere, and Arthur. At the conclusion of the "Book of Sir Tristram," the birth of Lancelot's son Galahad links this central division with the last major segment of the *Morte Darthur*. This final division runs from the quest of the Holy Grail through the increasingly narrower escapes from detection of Lancelot and Guinevere, to Arthur's final combat with the usurper Mordred and the "dolorous death and departing out of this world" of them all.

An outline of this basic three-part organization indicates the fundamental shape of the *Morte Darthur*. It hardly does justice, though, to the complexities of Malory's plot connections and excisions. Malory throughout his work struggled to simplify what Caxton tells us had become an almost unmanageable mass of accumulated Arthurian materials. Since Malory has become our standard history of Arthur, we tend to assume that he included everything available on the subject, or at least, everything important at his disposal. Only on an attentive reading do his surprising omissions become obvious. Perhaps what he leaves out says as much about the character of Malory's work as what he keeps.

In the first place, Malory eliminated much of the French material as it related to Merlin. Neither Merlin's supernatural birth and his independent adventures nor the titillating details of his pursuit of the maiden Malory calls "Nynyve" obtain much attention in the *Morte Darthur*. Malory's treatment of Merlin's entrapment by her could be described as the curtest on record. Merlin appears at the outset of book 1 as a figure whose prior history is recognized and ignored in the interest of concentration on Arthur. Under this restained treatment, the powerful figure of the king's wizard counselor is kept from dominating the narrative, unlike many later works.[26]

Other excisions from the French cycle tradition seem to have been made in the interest of clarity as well as of plot development. The duplicate Guinevere who beguiles Arthur in the prose *Lancelot* disappears. Though Spenser seems to have liked the general idea and uses it in the next century in his *Faerie Queene,* Malory evidently did not.[27] His decision to suppress altogether the thirteenth-century romance's account of the onset of the love affair between Lancelot and Guinevere is perhaps the most radical of his cuts. Its effect is to prevent most English-speaking readers from quite understanding a key passage of Dante's *Inferno.* Some of the most memorable plot material of Malory's thirteenth-century source vanishes in the process, and, with it, the role of Galahalt the Haut Prince as go-between in the matter, and the famous first kiss that inspired Dante's Paolo and Francesca.[28] Instead, Malory keeps the nature of the queen's interest in the chief knight of the Round Table ambiguous through much of the *Morte Darthur,* delaying his portrayal of the affair's consummation until well within a hundred pages of the end of the volume.

Since Malory left no commentary on his decisions, critics can only speculate as to his motives. In general, the effect of Malory's presentation seems to be to heighten our respect for King Arthur and for the lovers. He focuses readers' attention on the psychology of the fully developed chivalric love attachment—in the case of Lancelot and Guinevere—as it matures to face considerable social and religious stress. In the complementary case of Tristram and Isolde, Malory describes the opening of the story in detail, betraying a sceptical attitude to their magic love potion, and relegating its renowned and tragic conclusion to a brief secondhand report, perhaps for fear that it would overshadow his main ending. These decisions seem to reflect the author's sense of economy, balance, and the superior prestige of Camelot over Cornwall, "for the honour of bothe courtes be nat lyke" (Vinaver, 276). The foil is never allowed to upstage the protagonist.

This brief discussion of a few of Malory's most famous omissions reveals, most of all, that Malory was far from being a thoughtless compiler. His instinct was not to pack every available Arthurian legend into one book, but to shape his account of Arthur's world intelligently, even if it meant the sacrifice of some good stories. He treats his inherited materials with respect, but also with a deceptive degree of freedom, rearranging, interpreting, or adding as he thinks best. Like many other medieval authors, Malory often downplays his most startling innovations by disguising them as direct translations from some authoritative source. Whenever Malory announces that "the French book" mentions some detail, it usually means he made it up himself.

Besides numerous additions of details, clarifications, or personal comments, current critical opinion holds that Malory seems to have invented
at least two key episodes in his history of Arthur. At any rate, no
precise source has yet been found for either of them. The first apparently
new tale is that of Sir Gareth of Orkney, which follows immediately
on Malory's "Noble Tale of Sir Lancelot du Lake" and precedes the
"Book of Sir Tristram." It is therefore the last item in the first of
Malory's three major divisions, a significant location. Aspects of Gareth's
tale do have precedents in earlier romance. The hero is clearly a "fair
unknown" like the *bel inconnu* Guinglain in the French romance *Le
Bel inconnu,* who turns out to be Gawain's son, or like "La Cote Male
Tayle" from the Vulgate Cycle, whose tale Malory tells as one of the
adventures in his "Tristram."[29] Gareth, much like these predecessors,
is a young, nameless hero who appears at Arthur's court, is ridiculed
by the perennially abrasive Sir Kay, but goes on to succeed in defeating
several proven opponents to rescue a lady and become worthy of a
place at the Round Table. Malory's Gareth has a refreshingly innocent
quality that later appealed to Tennyson. Gareth turns out to be Arthur's
nephew, Gawain's youngest brother, for Malory the most likable member
of that vengeful family. The tale shows the young Round Table at its
best, inspiring even a member of the incorrigible "Orkney clan" to
higher chivalric ideals.

The second of Malory's inventions, the "Healing of Sir Urry," is
inserted in an even more striking position, after the episode of "The
Knight of the Cart," and immediately before Mordred and Agraivaine
denounce Lancelot and Guinevere to Arthur. One student has described
the tale of Sir Urry as Malory's attempt to give his favorite knight,
Sir Lancelot, his own Holy Grail. The Hungarian knight Sir Urry can
only be healed of his wounds by the best knight of all the world. The
attempts of Arthur and all the knights of his court to heal him give
Malory occasion to marshal an impressive catalogue of his chivalric
heroes just before internal conflict destroys their unity forever. A comparison of this list with the long list of Arthur's followers in the Welsh
Culhwch and Olwen shows how much the court of Arthur has changed
in five centuries. Lancelot's last-minute arrival, his acute embarrassment,
the genuine modesty of his prayer—"And Thou Blyssed Trynyte, Thou
mayste yeff me power to hele thys syke knyghte by the grete vertu
and grace of The, but, Good Lorde, never of myselff" (Vinaver, 668)—
and his shock at its successful result allow us to see him at his best
on the verge of his disgrace.

In the episodes that precede and follow Sir Urry's, Malory had at last reluctantly come to grips with the physical fact of the adultery of Lancelot and Guinevere. He had also described the last and most equivocal of the judicial duels in which Lancelot defends the queen from increasingly justifiable charges. "Sir Urry" rescues the frustrated idealist, Lancelot, from an unbroken slide into hypocrisy. We know he has fallen away from his promise on the grail quest to avoid Queen Guinevere as much as he can. Here Malory reasserts Lancelot's superiority to the other knights of the Round Table and to Arthur himself. Notably, the superiority he wants to emphasize in "Sir Urry" is not physical but spiritual. In the face of his mortifying state of deadly sin, Malory's Lancelot is still singled out for a special sign of God's grace. No wonder he weeps "as he had bene a chylde that had bene beatyn." What could have been a degrading revelation of his shame has become an unexpected victory.

This discussion of "Sir Urry" brings up the question of Malory's skill in maintaining the movement and variety of his narrative. This single, short episode illustrates his ability to build tension, even using stock devices like the catalogue of Arthur's knights as a technique of suspense. Yet much of the debate over Malory's talent as a writer has historically been concerned with his ability to tie narrative materials together. Certainly readers who expect to find in the *Morte Darthur* a work with the pace and logic of a novel are always disappointed. The *Morte Darthur* does not operate according to the laws established by Dickens, or by Virginia Woolf, for that matter. At the same time, it cannot claim the streamlined organization of a brief, single-stranded romance like *Sir Gawain and the Green Knight*.

Larry D. Benson's comparison of the *Morte Darthur* to a variety of prose romances other than its main thirteenth-century sources has been more illuminating than most critical discussions of this problem. His and other studies of Malory's technique as a storyteller reveal that the fifteenth-century writer had his own ideas about narrative momentum. Where his thirteenth-century French sources reveled in *entrelacement,* interweaving on occasion a surprising number of plots all going on at the same time, Malory preferred to eliminate many of his sources' shifts from one plot line to another in favor of more linear narrative development.[30] The classic "interlace structure," in which a story might shift at strategic moments between the adventures of two or three heroes, was never as popular in England as on the Continent.[31] It appears most noticeably in the central "Tristram" segment of the *Morte Darthur,* and in the *Quest of the Holy Grail,* both based on thirteenth-century French originals. Even in these sections, though, Malory has abbreviated or disentangled more complex presentations in the interest of a swifter, more direct account of the action. This is still not the plot organization modern readers are accustomed to, of course.

The *Morte Darthur* gave Malory the advantage of natural biographical unity, though he violates it slightly in the end to chronicle the fates of Arthur's surviving knights, especially Lancelot. Because Malory wrote at the end of the medieval explosion of interest in the Arthurian legend, he had a great deal more to include than simply the life of one man. Geoffrey of Monmouth offers a compact account of Arthur, king and conqueror, within the context of a legendary history of Britain that also included Lear and Brutus.[32] His Arthurian material comprises only one-tenth of Malory's book. The amount of additional information with which Malory had to cope bears witness to the magnetic attraction Arthur exerted on unrelated legends, histories, and new fictional ideas throughout the Middle Ages. It also posed severe organizational problems for the fifteenth-century writer. Massive prose cycles like the Vulgate Cycle lay beyond the scope of any normal author; scholars now believe it to be a collaborative work.[33] Such extended cycles were also passing out of fashion in terms of general scale, and, as we have seen, in terms of narrative technique. Malory's solution was to preserve some of the spirit, and certainly much of the plot, while abridging, defining, and reordering it to produce a more straightforward narrative in the style of his own day. The result is clearly quicker paced, less decorative or conversational, but more dramatic.

Malory's Prose Style

A sharpened sense of drama distinguishes Malory's work. This seems most vivid in his handling of dialogue, as he envisions clashes of character. If he excises much of the way of monologue, conversation, and description from his sources, the settings and speeches he does include bring Arthur's court unforgettably to life. Some credit should go to Malory's skill in imagining scenes, some to the force of his colloquial language, and some, of course, to the psychological truth of his characterizations. Of these, the first two skills bring him into correspondence with the fifteenth-century theater, where a few properties or a sketchily indicated setting, and direct, lively dialogue often made the play.

The contrast between Malory's methods of describing a locale or costume and the lavish details of contemporary records of tournaments or princely feasts is arresting. Where the heralds preserve the gold, velvet, plumage, tassels, and banners of late medieval chivalric display, Malory gives us a fountain in a forest clearing, a hall, the blazons of one or two important shields, a room in a tower.[34] This simplicity prevents us from deflecting our attention even for a moment from the predicaments of Malory's characters. Rarely is a personage or object described in visual terms unless the situation absolutely demands it. We learn more about Lancelot's physical appearance during his period of insanity, when it becomes important to the plot, than we do at any time earlier in the volume. Malory never offers his audience a static portrait of that preeminent knight, or of Arthur or Guinevere. One of the delights of reading the *Morte Darthur* is the almost unlimited scope Malory allows his audience's imagination to visualize all the familiar Arthurian characters as we see fit. Controversial decisions like Tennyson's to make Lancelot dark-haired, or T. H. White's to make him ugly, do not pique us here. This restraint in description is one of the hallmarks of Malory's style. It cuts him off at once from his great predecessor, the *Gawain* poet, and from his nineteenth-century admirers Tennyson and the Pre-Raphaelites, who all rejoiced in the lavish possibilities for descriptive detail that the Arthurian legend provided. Malory's decision to minimize description does make his work astonishingly spartan. Sometimes the unworked surface appears thin, or even threadbare. But the freedom from the heavy embroidery of some of his sources allows Malory an ease of movement that few of his precursors were able to achieve.

Malory's cleaner narrative line and sparing use of decor is complemented by his choice of direct language. Readers are sometimes startled by the freshness of a casual phrase thrown away by one or the other of Malory's characters. Who would have guessed how much of today's everyday speech goes back to 1460? When Sir Lambegus warns Sir Palomedes the Saracen that "what thou metyste with sir Trystrames thou shalt have both thy hondys full!" (Vinaver, 265) we are very much at home. Even when the language seems most archaic to us, it keeps a natural cadence that echoes the normal speech of Malory's day, whether in casual exchanges or in considered eloquence to meet the demands of a crisis.[35] This is one of the reasons that modernized editions of Malory find it so difficult to capture the effect of the original. Few writers in any language have been more versatile than Malory in their handling of the whole range of human communication.

Malory's most unforgettable scenes are built by meshing appropriate voices, language, and dramatic situation. The great farewell scenes of Arthur and the last knight to survive the battle with Mordred, Sir Bedevere, or of Lancelot and Guinevere, have often been praised. Less familiar moments are equally effective. The ill-starred knight with the Two Swords, Balin, fights to the death with his brother Balan; Malory dramatizes their horrified recognition of one another as they lie mortally wounded. Lancelot's shock at the healing of Sir Urry, and Gawain's entirely human disgust at his own abject failure in the quest of the Holy Grail might also be singled out for their revelations of character and economy of presentation.

As the variety of these examples may suggest, the society Malory depicts is by no means blackened by clouds of impending doom. There is a great deal of dry wit, and some high comedy, in the *Morte Darthur,* although, paradoxically, for us the funniest character in Malory may also be one of the most vile, King Mark of Cornwall, that unabashed and resourceful arch coward. Malory's finely tuned sense of drama never turns to tragedy, though the *Morte Darthur* describes some of the most painful events in our literature. As Benson has remarked, this may be because Malory did not believe in irrecoverable tragedy. The Christian Middle Ages, even as late as the fifteenth century, still saw life as a divine comedy of some kind, and the universe as one in which men and women of good will could be saved.[36] It is easy for modern readers to applaud Caxton's description of the *Morte Darthur:* "For herein may be seen noble chyvalrye, curtosye, humanyte, frendlynesse, hardynesse, love, friendshyp, cowardyse, murdre, hate, vertue, and synne" (Vinaver, xv). Perhaps more than anything else, it is the infinite variety of Malory's work that makes Arthur's England a world readers still delight to enter.

Malory has received perhaps his highest praise for the psychological truth of his characterizations. Surveying earlier Arthurian legends and literature reveals a few of the established traditions Malory inherited. They were not always helpful, of course; for one thing, they were often contradictory. From the first, Arthur was remembered for his generosity. He was also ruthless as a conqueror, in the chronicle tradition, and ineffectual as a husband, for Chrétien de Troyes and his French successors.[37] How could these traits be reconciled in one character? Kay, Arthur's companion as early as *Culhwch and Olwen,* appears both as a hero of supernatural abilities and as a tiresomely unpleasant and touchy person, a combination that was of interest to Steinbeck.[38] These inconsistencies in the portrayal of prominent Arthurian characters perhaps annoy the twentieth-century reader more than they did those of earlier periods, not because our aesthetic sensibilities are so much higher, but because we value consistency so highly. If a character changes, we want to know why. Hence, later retellings of the Arthurian legend are frequently encumbered with dutiful explanations. In fact, such clashing elements of character often lend many early Arthurian figures their fascination.

We can see this best, possibly, in Malory's Gawain, constructed from two warring traditions that the fifteenth century inherited. Throughout the Middle Ages, the English preserved the image of Arthur's nephew Sir Gawain as a paragon of courtesy, elegance, and prowess.[39] Perhaps from an origin as a sun god, Gawain's strength was reputed in some accounts to increase throughout the morning, until by noon it was three times greater than normal, waning again in the afternoon.[40] The French cycle romances gradually undermine this formidable reputation, replacing Gawain by their preferred hero Lancelot as the chief knight of the Round Table. The Gawain of the French prose romances is, like all his brothers except Malory's favorite, Gareth, an assassin given to secret gang attacks to carry out family vendettas. On his own account, he becomes the most promiscuous womanizer of Arthur's court.[41] The fourteenth-century English *Gawain* poet chose to follow the English tradition while playing with Gawain's dubious French reputation. Malory's Gawain combines both French and English character traits to make up a wonderfully jarring portrait that flaunts Gawain's most winning and most repellent features. The proud new knight we first meet plotting revenge with his younger brother travels on to a bewildering humiliation on his first quest. His accidental slaughter of a lady leads naturally to his penance, imposed by Queen Guinevere, of lifelong "service" to all ladies, a duty Gawain interprets rather more lavishly than the queen had presumably intended.[42] Malory depicts Gawain as a man for whom family loyalties are paramount. This explains the closeness of his bond to his maternal uncle Arthur, and the unreasoning fervor of his craze for revenge against his friend Lancelot after Lancelot has, by mischance, killed Gareth in a last effort to rescue Guinevere from the stake.[43]

The depth of Malory's understanding of the human spirit never lets him lose sight of Gawain's good qualities, even while Gawain's adherance to a code older than Christianity or chivalry is splitting Arthur's Round

Table. Among Malory's principal additions to the final section of the *Morte Darthur* is the text of Gawain's letter requesting Lancelot's forgiveness, and imploring him to return from his kingdom in France to help Arthur in the battle against Mordred. Gawain's lapses throughout the *Morte Darthur* can be deplorable, but he always manages to retrieve himself. Here the letter operates like a last confession. The frankness of his admission of wrongdoing provides a final glimpse of the Gawain who deserved to be, for Arthur, "the man in the worlde that I loved moste" (Vinaver, 709). Nowhere more clearly than in Gawain do we see good and evil, nobility and baseness, intertwined to make up a believable human being, and nowhere else is Malory's masterful handling of his Arthurian inheritance more brilliantly revealed.

There is no doubt that if Malory's characters reveal their believable humanity to us as if by magic on many occasions, there are also instances when changes in social custom or accepted modes of behavior shock us out of all sympathy with them. Masculine emotions may seem especially out of kilter. Heroes given to periodic fainting fits, tears, or running mad in the woods can strike the twentieth-century reader as more operatic than natural. Certainly one school of chivalric romance often heightened its characters' emotions for effect, sometimes mistaking hysteria for sublimity.[44] The idea that suffering is an ennobling experience, to be demonstrated graphically, was hardly confined to the Middle Ages. It is equally true that social conventions have changed more than once since the fifteenth century where the proper expression of emotional states is concerned. If a weeping hero evokes more embarrassment than compassion in the modern reader, this is hardly Malory's fault. Still, if fifteenth-century characters were given a surprising degree of liberty to express their feelings when the occasion demanded it, they were also expected to maintain an extraordinary reserve at other times. The extreme tension of controlling passions that must be concealed at all costs, balancing incompatible loyalties, and accepting the shame of a betrayal that is no fault of his own causes Lancelot's breakdown when Guinevere banishes him unjustly.[45] As a rule, the demands of a dramatic plot justify the most extreme psychological reactions that Malory chooses to present. The force of his imagination carries the sceptical reader beyond disbelief to comprehension of these almost incommunicable depths of human feeling.

The psychology of Malory's female characters has been unfairly neglected in altogether too much criticism of the *Morte Darthur*.[46] This situation probably reflects the assumption that the chivalric tradition is the exclusive preserve of the male sex, a bourne where women intrude only as rewards or educational devices. So it seems worth noticing the care Malory expends on drawing a variety of major female characters throughout the *Morte Darthur.*

The first sign of Malory's distinctive touch appears in the opening of book 1, with his introduction of Duchess Igraine of Cornwall, "a fair lady and a passynge wyse" (Vinaver, 3). In other tellings of the same story, Igraine is a passive victim of King Uther Pendragon's lust and Merlin's magic.[47] Malory makes her a comparatively active figure from the start. It is she who observes King Uther's attentiveness and demands that her husband Gorlois leave the court with her at once. "I suppose that we were sente for that I sholde be dishonoured. Wherfor, husband, I counceille yow that we departe from hens sodenly, that we may ryde all nyghte unto oure owne castell" (Vinaver, 3). As in Geoffrey of Monmouth's narrative, Igraine is trapped by Merlin's stratagem of disguising Uther as the absent Gorlois. After Uther leaves, Igraine learns that Gorlois had been killed before her visitors arrived. She reacts to the mystery of her visitor not with clamor but with pensive silence. In a perplexing and humiliating fix, pregnant with Arthur, Igraine keeps the dignity of a great lady.

The same poise without the moral balance reveals itself in Morgan le Fay the sorceress, Igraine's younger daughter by her first husband. She is her half-brother Arthur's nemesis on and off throughout his career, though at the end she appears among the ladies who carry the wounded king away in their barge to the Isle of Avalon for healing. Morgan reappears all through the *Morte Darthur,* always plotting against Arthur. Her qualities as a schemer appear at their most elaborate in the episode of "Arthur and Accolon."[48] There she is shown staging a duel between her hated half-brother the king and her current lover, Sir Accolon. Accolon has been given Arthur's stolen sword, Excalibur, with its sheath that prevents the wearer from losing any blood. Morgan has craftily substituted a much inferior replica with Arthur. Luckily, the damsel Nynyve, Merlin's bane, foils the plot. Meanwhile, back at her castle, Morgan is proceeding to implement the second phase of her design by murdering her husband, King Urience. She sends a maiden to fetch that king's own sword with notable coolness. "Go fecche me my lordes swerde, for I sawe never bettir tyme to sle hym than now" (Vinaver, 90). Evidently, for Morgan, part of the elegant design is that each king shall die by his own weapon. The damsel has the wit to inform Morgan's son Uwaine in time. When interrupted, Morgan excuses

herself with a plea of diabolical prompting. Even the news of her lover's
death does not shake her self-possession, though she is stricken by it.
With all her plots revealed, she still contrives to strike back by stealing
Excalibur's scabbard once more, and sends the vaunting message back
to her baffled pursuers, "Tell hym I feare him nat whyle I can make
me and myne in lyknesse of stonys, and lette hym wete I can do much
more whan I se my tyme" (Vinaver, 95).

The *Morte Darthur*'s later studies in female psychology show Malory
exploring the range and varying expressions of feminine love. His shrewd
recognition of female passion may perhaps have shocked Roger Ascham,
the humanist scholar who was to condemn the contents of Malory's
book as "open manslaughter and bold bawdry"; it certainly did startle
the Victorians, who took care to expurgate their schoolboys' editions of
the *Morte Darthur*.[49] Physical love in Malory ranges from the piratical
sensuality of Morgan and her sister sorceresses to the gleeful possessiveness
of that virtuous young lady Elaine the mother of Galahad, the first of
Malory's two Elaines, who twice employs her governess to bewitch Sir
Lancelot into bed with her. Malory also has his virgins, among them
Sir Percival's sister, the strict young nun of the quest of the Holy Grail,
and his second Elaine, Elaine of Astolat, whose fatal adoration of
Lancelot is aptly compared by her brother Sir Lavaine with his own
hero-worship. It is Elaine of Astolat who, in a famous passage, speaks
from her deathbed to defend human love. "Why sholde I leve such
thoughtes? Am I nat an erthely woman? And all the whyle the brethe
ys in my body I may complayne me, for my belyve ys that I do none
offence, though I love an erthely man, unto God, for he fourmed me
thereto, and all maner of good love comyth of God. And othir than
good love loved I never sir Launcelot du Lake" (Vinaver, 639). All
these ladies are simple by comparison with Queen Guinevere, frozen
at her first appearance, but thawing into majesty, laughter, jealous fury,
sangfroid, misery, tenderness, cruelty, self-sacrifice, and, in the end, the
grave discipline of renunciation.

Arthurian Chivalry in the *Morte Darthur*

The *Morte Darthur* has as often been arraigned for immorality as
praised for its high ethical standards. Roger Ascham's sixteenth-century
censure of its sex and violence has already been mentioned. A hundred
years earlier, Caxton was shrewd enough to warn his customers that
the book he had printed described an abundance of good and evil

conduct. Where another writer might have stressed the rule of divine providence by emphatically rewarding virtue and striking down sin, Malory can be as ambiguous as life itself. Belief in chivalry as a positive force in the world is one of the main premises of the Round Table's foundation. Arthur's knights swear: "Never to do outerage nothir mourthir, and allwayes to fle treson, and to gyff mercy unto hym that askith mercy . . . and allwayes to do ladyes, damesels, and jantilwomen and wydowes [socour] . . . uppon payne of dethe. Also, that no man take no batayles in a wrongefull quarell for no love ne for no worldis goodis" (Vinaver, 75). Arthur is held up for praise as an example of these and other knightly virtues, "for all knyghtes may lerne to be a knyght of hym" (Vinaver, 453). Failures to live up to the code are rebuked impressively. " 'What?' " seyde sir Launcelot, " 'is he a theff and a knyght? And a ravyssher of women? He doth shame unto the Order of Knyghthode, and contrary unto his oth. Hit is pyte that he lyvyth!' " (Vinaver, 160). The unchivalric knight is a menace to society at large, an offence to God, and to his own order. Yet chivalric morality is never presented as the only solution to life's problems, nor as an uniformly successful one. Dodging in and out among the trees all through the "Book of Sir Tristram" is the invulnerably antichivalric Sir Brunes sanz Pitie, disorderly, treacherous, cowardly, and given to riding down and trampling his opponents.[50] As far as we know, he suffers none of the agonies of remorse that overtake King Arthur's band of idealists, and apparently rides off into the sunset at the end absolutely intact. We may hope that he comes to a bad end, but Malory never documents it. There are problems that chivalry cannot solve—the quest of the Holy Grail, for one. There are others that it creates for itself: the "Book of Tristram" is full of purely chivalric dilemmas.

In the *Morte Darthur,* the chivalric ideal is only self-critical up to a point, though Malory recognizes its vulnerable spots. Sir Dinadan, the gadfly of the French prose *Tristan,* is softened in Malory from a character whose deflating comments raise more than a few blisters at King Arthur's court to one whose real loyalty to the chivalric code is never in doubt, however much he scoffs at love and the odd doings of knights-errant.[51] Malory reacts to attacks on knighthood in his sources by shielding his favorite institution as much as he can. As we have seen, the original quest of the Holy Grail, *La Queste del Saint Graal,* seems to have been written to demolish chivalry as a code of conduct by setting it against strict monastic values. It pulverizes the adulterous Lancelot, sinning with his liege lord's wife, beneath a series of ponderous sermons.[52]

Malory's Lancelot nevertheless comes out of the grail quest only just short of the three chosen grail knights, escaping a good deal of the chastisement that the French text had provided for his benefit, and gaining the sympathies of an audience that could identify with a sinner struggling to reach God. As Gawain says, " 'he ys as we be but if he take the more payne uppon hym' " (Vinaver, 558).

We glimpse Malory's true moral stance as an author best in those moments when he allows himself to speak to us directly. On occasion his messages are personal, when he requests our prayers for his "good deliverance" from prison, or sympathizes with Sir Tristram's illness in captivity, "and that ys the grettist payne a presoner may have" (Vinaver, 333). Generations of Malory's critics have recognized these statements as representing the voice of the author's own experience, the authentic comment of the knight prisoner. The same reaction has been recorded to Malory's praise of Sir Tristram as the inventor of hunting terms and methods useful to all gentlemen, "that all maner jantylmen hath cause to the worldes ende to prayse sir Trystram and to pray for his soule. AMEN, SAYDE SIR THOMAS MALLEORRE" (Vinaver, 416).

Malory the political commentator appears in his censure of the English for their disloyalty to Arthur when Mordred has siezed the throne, and for their general political unreliability. "Lo ye all Englysshemen, se ye nat what a myschyff here was? For he that was the moste kynge and nobelyst knyght of the world . . . and yet myght nat thes Englyshemen holde them contente with hym. Lo thus was the olde custom and usayges of thys londe, and men say that we of thys londe have nat yet loste that custom. Alas! thys ys a greate defaughte of us Englysshemen, for there may no thynge us please no terme" (Vinaver, 708). It is a complaint that might have been heard in Malory's time from either camp during the Wars of the Roses, though, as noted, some scholars have detected a Lancastrian bias in the *Morte Darthur*.[53]

On a more individual level, Malory bolsters his complex treatment of Guinevere with a surprising critique of the impatient lovers of his own age, with their urge for instant sexual gratification. "And ryght so faryth the love nowadayes, sone hot sone colde. . . . But the olde love was nat so. For men and women coulde love togedirs seven yerys, and no lycoures lustes was betwyxte them, and than was love trouthe and faythefulnes" (Vinaver, 649). Here Malory stresses loyalty and "stability" again, but as major virtues in love. Her constancy as a "true lover" is, Malory tells us, the virtue that redeems that difficult woman, Queen Guinevere.

In Malory's fictional universe, adherence to the chivalric virtues never ensures unlimited earthly success. But it does lead eventually to a final state bordering on popular canonization. The care Malory takes to inform us of the heavenly reception accorded to Galahad, Lancelot, and even Gawain, bears witness to the author's more or less qualified approval of his characters' lives or deaths: it is Gawain's confession that really saves him. The contradictory list of chivalric virtues that the devastated Sir Ector showers on his dead brother Lancelot signals to us the nobility and perhaps the impossibility of Malory's code of ethics. "Thou sir Launcelot, there thou lyest, that thou were never matched of erthely knyghtes hande. And thou were the curtest knyght that ever bare shelde! And thou were the truest frende to thy lovar that ever bestrade hors, and thou were the trewest lover, of a synful man, that ever loved woman, and thou were the kyndest man that ever strake wyth swerde" (Vinaver, 725). The high order of knighthood demands at once physical prowess, courtesy, truth in love and friendship, tenderness, humility, gentleness, and violence, all united in one person. Life in Malory's Arthurian England is indeed a test of character, though for some of the questions it poses there are no satisfactory answers. Lancelot's lifelong problem lies in his desperate attempt to reconcile incompatible demands placed on him by chivalry, feudalism, and Christianity, to serve his king, his lady, and God with equal loyalty. Precisely because he loves Guinevere, the noblest lady of England, his lord's wife, the attempt is perilous and success fleeting. It is his aspiration that makes Lancelot such an appealing character for Malory. As a human being, he appreciates Lancelot's struggle with his own passions.

The philosophy of the *Morte Darthur* is not ascetic or rarefied, mystical or romantic. Its narrative makes no pretense to allegorical or didactic rigor. Sir Philip Sidney once commented, perhaps as a retort to Roger Ascham, "Honest King Arthur can never displease a soldier."[54] It still seems the best reply to those who wish that Malory's story of King Arthur provided strict moral lessons. Malory's deep understanding of human ambitions and failures helped him to remake his Arthurian materials so that they appeal to an adult experience of an uncertain world.

Four and a half centuries before Tolkien's *Lord of the Rings,* Malory created for his readers a satisfying and coherent imaginary world. The sweep of its wide horizon takes in an immense range of human types. Above the ritualized violence of its combats, we see the fifteenth-century author gauging the clash of our passions and their impact for good and evil in "this world unstable."

In view of the magnitude of Malory's achievement, it hardly seems fair that he should remain the least respected of all major British writers. For too long the power of the Arthurian legend itself has received credit for the longevity of interest in the *Morte Darthur*. Malory is still seen far too often as a conduit, or perhaps as a laborious bricklayer whose chief merit lies in mortaring his sources together for posterity to unearth and remodel at will. The legend of Arthur unquestionably brought its own inspiration to Malory, as it had to Geoffrey of Monmouth, and as it would to Tennyson and T. H. White. Malory did not invent the majority of his characters, nor their fates. But he did bring to the legend of Arthur a majesty no other writer has yet conferred upon it.

While trying to encompass in one short chapter both the nature of Malory's greatness and his place in Arthurian literature, I have repeated much that has been said by others. I have also left out much that should have been said, and my notes and bibliography can only begin to suggest sources for further information. Perhaps, though, the best advice to readers regarding the "knight prisoner" and his book is William Caxton's counsel to his contemporaries that they forget trivial everyday preoccupations and "Leve this. Leve it and rede the noble volumes of Saynt Graal, of Lancelot, of Galaad, of Trystram . . . of Gawayn and many mo. Ther shalle ye see manhode, curtosye and gentylnesse."[55]

Chapter Four
Arthur through 1900

The authors of romances were not the only medieval contributors who carried forward the story of King Arthur up to the Renaissance. From the thirteenth to the sixteenth century historians continued to puzzle over the question of Arthur's real existence or actual biography. The story of Arthur also adorned pageants and tournaments, as well as the visual arts, converging with the efflorescence of Arthurian drama proper in the sixteenth century. Arthur appeared among the Nine Worthies, the ubiquitous grouping of the nine greatest chivalric heroes of world history that was celebrated by authors and artists from the late thirteenth century on. These alternative channels of transmission became much more important in the sixteenth century as Renaissance authors re-evaluated their medieval inheritance.

This chapter begins by investigating some often neglected sixteenth and seventeenth-century Arthurian experiments, for the most part historical, epic, and dramatic works. It then moves through the eighteenth century to examine the return of interest in Arthur with the rise of the romantic movement and nineteenth-century medievalism. The main section of this chapter, though, is devoted to Arthurian literature from 1850 to 1900, its second great age.

Arthur in Sixteenth- and Seventeenth-Century England

The sixteenth- and seventeenth-century attempts to rework British legendary material using new media appropriate to the English Renaissance vary widely in their degree of success. Novelty, diversity, and experimental freedom with traditional materials characterize this relatively neglected phase of Arthurian literature. This was a period of strong Arthurian interest; King Arthur in fact became a controversial and difficult subject for Elizabethan, Jacobean, and Restoration authors. The foundation for this controversy was laid by the historians.

Arthur in Tudor history. Doubts concerning Arthur's real existence, or at least the historicity of his legend, were certainly current as early as the twelfth century. In his 1485 preface to Malory, William Caxton momentarily assumed the point of view of a skeptic, repeating the doubts voiced in Ranulf Higden's fourteenth-century *Polychronicon*. Many fifteenth-century Continental authors were even more dubious, their patriotism not being involved in the question.[1] Still, the best-known historical controversy over Arthur's existence remains the sixteenth-century debate between Polydore Vergil and John Leland.

The Italian humanist Polydore Vergil (c. 1470–1555) attracted the fury of patriotic English writers through his attacks on Geoffrey of Monmouth, "more a poet than an historian," in his *Anglica historia (History of England)*. The earliest manuscript of this work in the Vatican library has been dated around 1512–13, though the first edition did not appear until 1534.[2] Like Higden before him, Polydore Vergil questioned Geoffrey's account of Arthur's Continental campaigns; he also doubted the antiquity of Arthur's tomb. As he knew well, Vergil was on delicate ground: Henry VII had brought Arthur to the center of Tudor political propaganda. The Welsh origins of the Tudor dynasty led Henry VII to present himself and especially his eldest son, Prince Arthur, as successors of King Arthur, their dynasty the fulfillment of Merlin's prophecies of Arthur's return. The strong critical language of Vergil's manuscript *History* would not have been judicious to publish.

As it was, Polydore Vergil's skeptical remarks stung the patriotic antiquary John Leland (1503–52) to compose his combative 1544 *Assertio inclytissimi Arturii, regis Britanniae,* translated in 1582 by Richard Robinson as *A Learned and True Assertion of . . . Arthur*.[3] Leland excites the greatest interest today for his work as the antiquary to Henry VIII. He is on his strongest ground in the collection of physical evidence, not in historical analysis, which is Vergil's forte. His surveys of monastic libraries, many shortly destroyed in the dissolution of the monasteries, led to the preservation of a variety of manuscripts that otherwise might have been lost. Like Caxton, Leland cites Arthur's burial at Glastonbury, and describes the cross, now lost, that was found in the grave. He also examined "Arthur's seal" at Westminster, evidently the same object Caxton described in his preface to Malory.[4] His associations of Camelot with South Cadbury and of the Round Table at Winchester with the Round Table of Edward I and Mortimer have both proven longsighted. Otherwise his defense of Arthur is a partisan document; the immediate future lay with Polydore Vergil, whose skepticism is echoed in Milton's *History of Britain*. For political reasons, Roberta Brinkley suggests, Milton's history prefers to glorify the Saxons, seen as the developers of English law, learning, and representative government. Arthur's disorderly Britons were to become "a distant mirror" of the failing commonwealth.[5]

The Arthurian epic. The sixteenth- and seventeenth-century attempt to translate the legends of Arthur into the medium of the Renaissance epic is, with one major exception, a history of disappointment. There is no lack of admiration for the subject among the English poets. Michael Drayton's *Poly-Olbion* of 1612 remarked on the suitability of Arthur as an epic hero. For Ben Jonson, Arthur was the most promising topic available to an English epic poet. The narrative poem he announced to William Drummond never materialized, but Arthurian references elsewhere in Jonson's work suggest he knew the subject well.[6] As it is, his pageant, the *Speeches at Prince Henry's Barriers* remains Jonson's only surviving Arthurian work. The young John Milton's ambitious plan to write an epic poem on Arthur and his knights was replaced sometime between 1639 and 1658 by the biblical subject of *Paradise Lost*. His ultimate rejection of Arthur as a topic has preoccupied a number of critics. John Dryden, in Milton's wake, projected an Arthurian epic that he never found the leisure to carry out. Like Jonson, he gives us a glimpse of his Arthurian poetry in a dramatic work, his opera *King Arthur* of 1691.[7]

Of existing Arthurian epics, Edmund Spenser's *Faerie Queene* stands in the front rank as a poem, though not as a strictly Arthurian one. Spenser's Prince Arthur is meant to embody the separate virtues illustrated by his knights, together with the royal trait of magnanimity, "magificence." He reappears intermittently, among the adventures of other knights and ladies, in search of Gloriana, the "faerie queene" he is destined to marry. Besides the perfected English gentleman, Arthur represents the house of the Tudors, and Gloriana, Elizabeth I. Had Spenser completed the work he outlined in his letter to Raleigh, Arthur would presumably have been given a larger role to play. Still, it seems clear that Spenser, through the medium of the Italian Ariosto, is preserving the structure of the romance while discarding the traditional story, all but the figures of Arthur and Merlin. Arthur is, again, a background figure, if a majestic one; the foreground is occupied with the illustrative activities of his subordinate knights.[8]

The greatest disappointment of all for English readers may be provided by the one seventeenth-century poet who did complete not one but two Arthurian epics. *Prince Arthur* and *King Arthur,* the compositions of Sir Richard Blackmore (1654–1729), physician and poet, are practically indigestible, as well as unobtainable, today. Blackmore's works convert the Arthurian legend wholesale into political allegory complementing the reigning English monarchs, William and Mary. Arthur's Continental campaigns are remodeled in the image of William's. Drawing on Spenser, Tasso, Milton, and Dryden, Blackmore subjects Arthur to satanic temptation in book 6 of *King Arthur.* As Brinkley notes, this use of Arthur for contemporary allegory, as well as some important features of the plot, derives from Dryden, who was quick to resent Blackmore's adoption of his plan for an Arthurian epic, made more exasperating still by obvious borrowings from Dryden's opera *King Arthur.*[9]

While the epic poets struggled to adapt Arthur to the medium of Virgil, the romances remained surprisingly popular reading in Renaissance England. Louis B. Wright, W. Mead, and others have surveyed this aspect of sixteenth-century taste. Malory remained in print until 1634; new prose romances set in Arthurian England, like Richard Johnson's *Tom a Lincolne* (1599–1607), and Christopher Middleton's *Chinon of England* (1597), played on the continuing interest in the world of Arthur. Strictures like Roger Ascham's on the immorality of the *Morte Darthur,* and Nashe's 1589 slap at the Arthurian romances as the work of lazy monks expelled from monasteries also testify to the unabated appetite for tales of chivalric adventures of the Round Table, and bear witness to the perplexity and annoyance of many humanist authors at such unaccountably backward taste.[10]

In fact, in English, the great age of Arthurian narrative poetry did not arrive until the nineteenth century.

Arthurian drama, 1500–1900.   No account of Arthurian experiments between the sixteenth and the nineteenth centuries should omit Arthurian drama. Though the first English Arthurian play dates from the sixteenth century, Arthurian pageants were unquestionably popular in the Middle Ages. Many were dramatized tournaments or interludes devised to celebrate a knighting ceremony, coronation, or wedding. In England, Edward I's 1299 marriage was graced by a notable Round Table. Edward III also indulged in this type of entertainment. Pageants of the Nine Worthies with speeches by each chivalric hero have also been documented; Shakespeare parodies them in *Love's Labour's Lost.*[11]

The Arthurian tournaments and court pageants invited the audience to participate in the world of the Round Table, becoming part of an improvised drama. But the earliest surviving texts of Arthurian plays come from the sixteenth century. Besides the few dramatic works we still have, references in the Stationer's Register, Henslowe's diary, and other sources indicate that other Arthurian plays and masques were written and performed throughout the Elizabethan and Jacobean periods.[12]

The turmoil among historians and epic poets over the proper handling of the Arthurian romances left sixteenth- and seventeenth-century dramatists with two basic choices. Authors could choose to present the familiar legend as inherited from the Middle Ages, or they could alter it, sometimes radically, to suit a new audience. Of the four principal dramatic works to be discussed here, three preserve the recognizable legendary narrative, while the fourth breaks decisively with the established material.

The first in chronological order is Thomas Hughes's attempt to recast Arthur as a Senecan tragic hero, *The Misfortunes of Arthur.* The gentlemen of Grays Inn performed this lurid work before Queen Elizabeth I at Greenwich in 1588. Its acts are interspersed with "dumb shows" devised by a group of collaborators including Francis Bacon. These curious pantomimes foreshadowing and allegorizing the action yet to come may be the most astonishing feature of the work. Hughes's plot is based more or less on Geoffrey of Monmouth. Its principal characters are, once again, Guinevere, Mordred, and Arthur. Arthur's betrayal by his overindulged favorite, Mordred, provides lavish opportunities for magniloquent Senecan speeches. Meanwhile, the ghost of Gorlois, Duke of Cornwall, hovers around the scene, prophesying doom for Arthur in revenge for the loss of his wife Igerne to Uther Pendragon. The production ends with Arthur's dying speech, in which the king displays remarkable stamina recalling his foreign conquests and asking that his grave be concealed from posterity, to add to his fame.[13]

Ben Jonson wrote in *Speeches at Prince Henry's Barriers* for performance at court in January 1609 to mark James I's eldest son's first appearance in a tournament. It can be connected with the long line of Arthurian tournaments that stretch back to the early thirteenth century.[14] Jonson's pageant combines familiar Arthurian characters like the Lady of the Lake, Merlin, and Arthur himself with a personification, Chivalry, who is awakened from her sleep to open the gates of her ruined house, and so start the joust. The Lady releases Merlin from his tomb, where she formerly imprisoned him, paralleling the legend of Merlin and Nynyve in Malory. Arthur, "discovered in a starre above," sends down a shield for Prince Henry. Stellifying Arthur as Arcturus, and the shield's descent, are elegant classical variations on the original. The chivalry Merlin teaches Prince Henry in his speech is that appropriate to a peacetime ruler of England, enforced by historical examples from Richard I to James I. Merlin ends the tournament and the masque with a tribute to the royal family. Inigo Jones's surviving designs for the pageant allow modern audiences to glimpse the spectacle visually as well as verbally.[15]

William Rowley's *Birth of Merlin, or the Child Has Found His Father* was also ascribed by its publisher to Shakespeare, and some recent criticism does detect his hand in this play, published in 1662, but written perhaps forty years earlier.[16] The only one of the four dramas discussed here with no overt court connections, the *Birth of Merlin* approaches the Arthurian world in a more relaxed manner. Indeed, the birth of Merlin is presented as the comic subplot of the play. Serious young lovers brooding on the future of wartime Britain are continually interrupted by the Clown and his pregnant sister, Joan go to't, in search of the courtier who has seduced her. The newborn Merlin who eventually appears is a prodigy, complete with beard and book, and it is he who produces his father the devil for inspection. Merlin's last scene, in a more serious vein, brings him on to rescue his mother from the renewed attentions of his father. Having routed the devil, Merlin promises to erect Stonehenge as a monument to Joan. The *Birth of Merlin* follows the main lines of the Merlin legend as presented in Geoffrey of Monmouth and the French Merlin tradition. While the main plot is eminently forgettable, the Merlin story is handled with comic verve that makes this the most entertaining of the early Arthurian plays.

Dryden's 1691 "Dramatick Opera," *King Arthur,* strays furthest from the standard Arthurian narratives, preferring the company of Spenser, Tasso, and *The Tempest.* Henry Purcell provided the music, which is still well regarded and performed today.[17] Arthur and Merlin are the only two surviving traditional characters, though an Aurelius appears briefly as a "friend of Arthur." Dryden complained to the Marquis of Halifax in his dedicatory letter that the original script, written under Charles II, had to be greatly altered for performance under William and Mary. Dryden's earlier British play, *Albion and Albanius,* a prologue to *King Arthur,* offers some suggestions as to Dryden's earlier political allegory.[18] The 1691 opera's plot involves the rivalry of Arthur and the Saxon king of Kent, Oswald, for the hand of the blind princess Emmeline. Merlin aids Arthur, while a Saxon magician, Osmond, opposes them. A pair of spirits, Pilidel and Grimbald, serve as the Ariel and Caliban of the piece, which revels in stage machinery and special effects; Dryden comments, "these sorts of Entertainment are principally design'd for the Ear and Eye." From the descent of Merlin in a chariot drawn by dragons through Arthur's temptations in the Enchanted Wood, *King Arthur* is visually and aurally gorgeous. Dryden uses the blind princess and the enamored Saxon enchanter to some comic effect. Emmeline's naiveté seems to be modeled on that of Shakespeare's Miranda. *King Arthur* was successful enough as a theatrical spectacle to hold a place in the English dramatic repertoire from 1691 to 1842; its twentieth-century revivals have revealed its merits as theater.

The departure of Dryden's *King Arthur* from the stage coincides interestingly with the advent of the new Arthurian literature of the nineteenth century; after 1842, Emmeline is no longer a satisfactory substitute for Guinevere.

The Reemergence of Arthur: Nineteenth-Century Medievalism

With the approach of the nineteenth century, the incipient romantic movement began to resuscitate Arthur and Merlin from their pallid eighteenth-century afterlife as gilt on rather dusty theatrical gingerbread. The reaction against neoclassicism that animated the English romantics brought with it a renewed interest in the Middle Ages, and the medieval romance. The Gothic revival championed a medievalized aesthetic in art, architecture, and literature, as well as a drastic revision of historians' views of the Middle Ages. The birth of medieval studies as a discipline can be traced to this period: principal figures in its early development include Sharon Turner, Bishop Percy, the irascible Joseph Ritson, Walter W. Skeat, and F.J. Furnivall. Long neglected literature was at last reprinted, most significantly, Malory's *Morte Darthur*. It can be argued that the rediscovery of Malory triggered the nineteenth-century revival of English Arthurian literature. Sir Walter Scott, the Pre-Raphaelites, and Tennyson all drew on their reading of Malory for the basic Arthurian narrative they followed, as well as for much of their inspiration.

Alice Chandler has analyzed the social and historical factors that lay behind the medievalism of the nineteenth century. On the simplest level, a reaction against the industrialization and nineteenth-century urban social evils led authors and social reformers like William Cobbett, and later John Ruskin, to idealize the agrarian Middle Ages as a lost era of faith, order, and harmony.[19] Mark Girouard has illustrated and discussed the renewed nineteenth-century interest in chivalry as a useful parallel for the code of conduct expected of a Victorian gentleman.[20] The quests of Arthur's knights-errant were seen as vehicles of instruction in the manly virtures—courage, faith, sexual fidelity—in a way that recalls Spenser's recasting of romance as moral education. Arthurian love and religion were more complex problems for the nineteenth century. Individual writers would express their own reasons for taking up the subject of Arthur; their number and enthusiasm suggest that the legend has special meaning for this era.

Arthurian literature in the romantic period. Although the great surge of Arthurian literature did not arise until after 1850, a surprising number of romantic writers did try their hands at Arthurian poetry. Thomas Warton described Arthur's burial at Glastonbury as early as 1777 in "The Grave of King Arthur." Two romantic poets combined Arthurian characters with the favorite nineteenth-century fairy-tale plot of Sleeping Beauty, perhaps as a feminine variation on the "cave legend" or Merlin's tomb. William Wordsworth's "Egyptian Maid" of 1830 culminates in the unprecedented wedding of Sir Galahad with the Egyptian princess he has raised from an enchanted trance.[21] In Sir Walter Scott's "Bridal of Triermain" (1813) the sleeping princess is an illegitimate daughter of Arthur and the bloodthirsty enchantress Guendolen. Scott had previously edited the Middle English romance of *Sir Tristrem* from the Auchinleck Manuscript. His reading and appreciation of Malory are displayed in the prologue and notes to *Marmion* (1808). Scott's reading in medieval history and literature is wide ranging. In view of his superior knowledge of medieval and later Arthurian works, it is curious that Scott approaches the material so cautiously. The Arthurian core of his narrative poem "The Bridal of Triermain," is cushioned, first, by a contemporary frame in which the tale is told by an early nineteenth-century Arthur to his beloved Lucy, and then by an account of the Border knight Roland de Vaux, who is to reawaken Arthur's enchanted daughter. This procedure anticipates Tennyson's use of a modern frame for his 1842 "Morte d'Arthur." The pleasantly readable "Bridal of Triermain" is hardly on a level with Scott's more celebrated narrative poems, *Marmion* or *The Lady of the Lake*. The pageantry of its magical castle, supplied of course by Merlin, was admirably suited for theatrical presentation in the spectacular tradition of Dryden's *King Arthur*. The "Bridal of Triermain" in fact was reworked for the theater and performed successfully through the nineteenth century.[22]

Hookham Frere's unfinished ottava rima poem, "The Monks and the Giants" (1817–18), uses Arthurian characters as a vehicle for social satire; his work has been recognized as an important precursor of Byron's *Don Juan,* which it resembles in choice of traditional subject matter and technique.[23]

The Welsh tradition of Arthur also revived unexpectedly in Thomas Love Peacock's satirical novel *The Misfortunes of Elphin* of 1829. Peacock's protagonist, the bard Taliesin, rescues his master Elphin and Queen Guinevere from their imprisonment, as Peacock uses the Arthurian setting to ridicule his favorite nineteenth-century abuses. The *Misfortunes of Elphin* connects, on one side, with the fantastic Welsh tradition of *Culhwch and Olwen,* and on the other with Mark Twain's *Connecticut Yankee in King Arthur's Court.*[24]

Tennyson's *Idylls of the King*. After Malory's *Morte Darthur,* the most influential Arthurian work in English remains Alfred, Lord Tennyson's *Idylls of the King,* its continuing effect discernible, surprisingly on occasion, in the most self-consciously original twentieth-century Arthurian novels. On later Arthurian poetry, the hand of the *Idylls* is heavier still. After the feints of Jonson, Milton, and Dryden in the seventeenth century, Tennyson gave England its first Arthurian epic.

Alfred Tennyson was born in 1909 in Lincolnshire. His interest in Arthur apparently dated from childhood, when he first encountered Malory.[25] Tennyson studied at Trinity College, Cambridge, from 1827 to 1831; he and his brothers had already published a volume of their poetry early in April 1827. Alfred Tennyson's first independent book, *Poems, Chiefly Lyrical,* appeared in 1830. Severe reviews of this and his 1832 *Poems* distressed Tennyson; his reputation as a poet was consolidated with his *Poems* of 1842, *The Princess* of 1847, and most of all by *In Memoria* (1850), his volume of elegaic poetry in memory of his college friend Arthur Hallam. "Merlin and the Gleam," a later autobiographical poem of Tennyson's, associates Hallam with King Arthur. Tennyson succeeded Wordsworth as poet laureate in 1850. He accepted a barony, becoming Lord Tennyson, in 1883, and died on 6 October 1892.[26]

Tennyson's earliest published Arthurian poem, "The Lady of Shalott," appeared in his 1832 collection of poems. The last, "Merlin and the Gleam," was published in 1889. The dates illustrate the persistence of

Tennyson's interest in Arthur, from well before the publication of the first installment of his *Idylls of the King,* "Morte d'Arthur," in 1842. The 1842 volume also contained two shorter Arthurian pieces, "Sir Launcelot and Queen Guinevere," evidently planned as a companion to "The Lady of Shalott," and written in a similar stanzaic form, and "Sir Galahad," a companion to the non-Arthurian "St. Agnes."[27]

The "Morte d'Arthur" differs from the shorter poems in its close reliance on Malory. The "Lady of Shalott" and Merlin in "Merlin and the Gleam" both represent the poet. The Lady of Shalott's isolation in her tower permits her to create, while direct experience of reality, in the person of the innocent passerby Launcelot, brings on her death.

Tennyson published a number of political poems in 1852 under the pseudonym "Merlin." In "Merlin and the Gleam," the wizard himself describes his lifelong quest following "the Gleam," and elliptically touches on the major events of Tennyson's life.

The fragmentary "Sir Launcelot and Queen Guinevere" (1842) takes as its subject Launcelot's ride with Guinevere to her wedding with Arthur. Galahad is the speaker in "Sir Galahad," recounting his as yet incomplete quest for the Holy Grail. William Morris addressed the same subject in his 1859 "Sir Galahad: A Christmas Mystery."[28]

Tennyson presented the first installment of *Idylls of the King* in the 1842 volume with, for twentieth-century readers, astonishing diffidence. The "Morte d'Arthur," later revised as "The Passing of Arthur," the last in the *Idylls,* is here surrounded with a contemporary frame, in which a group of college friends meet at Christmas. The narrative of Arthur's last battle here figures as the eleventh book of an epic poem on Arthur, rescued from the flames when the poet, one of the young men present, burns the remainder of his manuscript. This expedient recalls Scott's framing of the "Bridal of Triermain." It allows Tennyson to voice doubts about the appropriateness of epic poetry and the subject of Arthur for a nineteenth-century audience. Over the short term, these doubts were justified. The discouraging reviews of John Sterling and Leigh Hunt did deter Tennyson from completing his projected epic at that time. Hunt's comment on the frame device were particularly shrewd.[29] A number of early manuscript sketches for a major Arthurian work, epic or dramatic, published by Hallam Tennyson, show Tennyson experimenting with the topic in the 1830s. He returned to Arthur, for him, still, "the greatest of all poetic subjects," later in the 1840s, traveling in Cornwall and Ireland in 1848 in search of material. In

1859 four idylls, "Enid," "Vivien," "Elaine," and "Guinevere," were published, and were well received; Arthur's hour had finally returned.[30]

Tennyson had worked out a plan for the complete series of poems, but did not supply the missing sections for some time; the Holy Grail in particular gave him pause as a subject to be approached with special care. The second group of idylls, "The Coming of Arthur," "The Holy Grail," "Pelleas and Ettarre," and "The Passing of Arthur," appeared in 1869. The three remaining sections, the "Last Tournament," "Gareth and Lynette," and "Balin and Balan," were published in 1871, 1872, and 1885, respectively.[31]

Serial publication was eminently familiar to nineteenth-century readers; Dickens's novels provide the best-known example of this practice. Tennyson's blank-verse idylls function admirably in their dual roles as self-contained poems and as elements in a larger work. Among the unifying factors that tie together the whole poem, the poet himself noted the cycle of the seasons. Arthur first appears on New Year's Eve and marries in the spring; the court sees the grail vision in summer, and the autumn scenes of the "Last Tournament" and Gunievere's flight to her abbey give way to the deep midwinter of Arthur's passing. The *Idylls* trace the rise of Arthur's kingdom from the first establishment of his ideals in the Round Table through the harmony of their brief fulfillment to disillusionment, decay, and a return to chaos. The "War of Soul and Sense," of reason struggling to conquer human appetites, had been associated with Arthur in Dryden's *King Arthur,* as his king surmounted the sensual temptations of the Enchanted Forest to win Princess Emmeline. The theme finds its definitive Arthurian expression in Tennyson's *Idylls* where the one sin of Lancelot and Guinevere rots at the heart of Arthur's ideal civilization.[32]

Tennyson resisted rigid allegorical or symbolic interpretation of his *Idylls.* He does see Arthur as an ideal figure, and portrays him as an exalted being of mysterious origins, more than once as an unmistakable type of Christ.[33] The idyll that opens the work, "The Coming of Arthur," considers and discards Geoffrey of Monmouth's story of Uther and Igerne as an unworthy tradition; he offers as an alternative a new tale that Merlin received the infant Arthur from the sea on the night of Uther's death, preceded by a vision of a dragon ship. The scene recalls the opening of *Beowulf,* with the infant king Scyld Scefing's arrival in Denmark and ship burial.[34] Other embarrassing legends disappear more completely still. Arthur's difficult half-sisters Morgan le Fay and Morgause vanish without a trace, replaced by Tennyson's

Bellicent, whose innocent narrative of her childhood companionship with Arthur is misconstrued by her evil-minded son Mordred. Any suggestion of sin on Arthur's part is hereby eliminated. The "Coming of Arthur" does convey a foreboding of doom, though no crime of Arthur's brings it on. Arthur's marriage with Guinevere, the main event of this idyll, is itself a fatal moment for those who know the story. The "deathless love" that Arthur swears both to his queen and to his best knight Lancelot, Lancelot's escorting Guinevere to her wedding, and Guinevere's failure to meet Arthur's eyes at their marriage ceremony all presage evil. Tension also derives from the clash between the animal brutality of the warfare that precedes Arthur and the chivalric vows to which Arthur binds his knights.

The image of Arthur enthroned amid his knights is developed further in the next idyll, "Gareth and Lynette," based on Malory's "Tale of Sir Gareth." Here Tennyson describes Camelot, an enchanted city "built to music" where Arthur dispenses his new justice. The reader sees this scene through the eyes of an enthralled new arrival, Gareth, Bellicent's youngest son. As in Malory, he conceals his identity and asks to spend a year and a day among Arthur's kitchen boys. Tennyson makes this odd request the stipulation of Gareth's mother, who hopes to keep her last son with her. Tennyson is also kind enough to release Gareth after a month in the scullery. Sir Kay, Arthur's seneschal, has the same satirical tongue as in earlier Arthurian literature. Launcelot discerns Gareth's true quality, but in Tennyson it is Arthur who knights him. The quest Gareth undertakes to prove his worth has also been reordered; the four knights he must conquer to release the imprisoned Dame Lyonors assume the names "Morning-star," "Noon-sun," "Evening-star," and "Death," symbolizing the course of human life. Gareth himself bears much the same steadfast character in Tennyson as in Malory; Tennyson differs by marrying him at the conclusion not to Lyonors, the lady in the tower, but to his guide, her sharp-tongued sister Lynette. "Gareth and Lynette" represents the springtide of Arthur's court, with fewer shadows than in any other idyll. Launcelot's nobility and friendship are as yet apparently untarnished, and Guinevere is strangely invisible.

The queen returns at the beginning of the next idyll, "The Marriage of Geraint," inspired by "Geraint" in Lady Charlotte Guest's translation of *The Mabinogion*. Tennyson was also acquainted with Chrétien de Troyes's *Erec and Enide,* which tells the same story.[35] Prince Geraint withdraws from court to protect his wife Enid from contamination, made suspicious by rumors of an affair between Lancelot and Guinevere. His suspicions fall next on Enid herself, through his misunderstanding of a speech he overhears, and he orders her to ride out on a quest to recover his lost fame. As Enid puts on her oldest dress, in a flashback Tennyson describes the hunt that leads Geraint to meet and win Enid in her impoverished father's hall. He jousts for her at the tournament of the Sparrowhawk, humbles the usurper Edyrn and regains Enid's father's earldom. The faded dress Enid wears to Arthur's court at Geraint's command is a test of her obedience, apparently forgotten by Geraint after their marriage.

"The Marriage of Geraint" and "Geraint and Enid," originally published as a single narrative, were divided in 1873. The second idyll takes up the story of Geraint's travels in the wilderness with Enid. He has ordered her to ride ahead and not to speak to him, an order she disobeys repeatedly to warn him of impending danger. Enid's loyalty is vindicated in the course of the quest, as much through her obedience as through her efforts to comply with Geraint's unreasonable demands. The episode ends with their reunion with Arthur, and with Arthur's veiled rebuke of Geraint.

"Balin and Balan" appears next in Tennyson's sequence, though it was the last idyll to be composed. The brother knights who kill one another derive from Malory, as does Balin's rash temper. Tennyson has stripped down the original tale of Balin's adventures still further. He interprets the castle of King Pellam, the grail castle in Malory, as a haunt of superstitious asceticism rather than in terms of any nobler spirituality of the grail; Tennyson has no use for the cult of relics. The evil Garlon is, again, Pellam's son.[36] The conversation between Guinevere and Launcelot that convinces Balin of the queen's impurity is an innovation of Tennyson's: the revelation of their sin drives him from the court that had begun to reform him, and eventually leads to his doom. Vivien, the wily damsel from King Mark's court who ensnares Merlin in the following idyll, is glad to confirm Balin's fears. In Malory, Balin's "dolorous stroke" with the spear of the Crucifixion wounded King Pellam and laid his country waste. In Tennyson, Balin employs the spear in his duel with his brother Balan. Their final interview restores Balin's faith in the queen he worshiped, though not the reader's. As they die, Vivien's mischievous journey continues toward Arthur's court.

"Merlin and Vivien" did not receive this title until 1870, but was written as early as 1856. Vivien, then named Nimuë, was originally meant to counterbalance Enid in the 1857 *Enid and Nimuë, the True and the False*.[37] Where in Malory and many French prose romances Viviane or Nynyve are to some extent positive characters, in Tennyson Vivien replaces Morgan le Fay as "the evil genius of the Round Table."[38] Raised at the court of the evil King Mark, she is not unexpectedly a total cynic, sent to the court of King Arthur to undermine its ideals. Failing to attract Arthur's attention, she attaches herself to Merlin, follows him to the forest of Brocéliande, and importunes him into revealing the spell that imprisons him forever. Vivien's weapon is her tongue; her venomous slander lashes everyone from the innocent Percivale to Lancelot and Guinevere, who indeed are guilty, as Merlin reluctantly admits. The insect and serpent imagery that Tennyson applies to Vivien links her voluble temptation of Merlin with the snake of Eden and with the ravening animal world of pre-Arthurian Britain. Malory's Nynyve is "passing weary" of Merlin's dangerous pursuit; Tennyson's Vivien reverses the process, wearing out the old wizard at last.

The following idyll, "Lancelot and Elaine," first appeared as "Elaine" in 1859. The story of Elaine of Astolat parallels that in Malory's *Morte Darthur* reasonably closely. In Malory, though, the episode occurs after the quest of the Holy Grail, while Tennyson places it immediately before the crucial event. Tennyson's innovations include the rationale for the tournament Lancelot is attending in disguise, a type of elaboration he provides again in "The Last Tournament." The diamonds Lancelot fights for were taken by Arthur from the crown of a skeleton king, who died killing his brother. The fact lends a sinister quality to the tournament. Tennyson stresses the contrast between the young and innocent Elaine's adoration of Lancelot and the bitter guilt of the relationship between Lancelot and Guinevere. Among Tennyson's alterations to the story is the omission of Elaine's deathbed declaration that "good love" comes from God—not perhaps considered a maidenly speech in the nineteenth century, whatever it may have been in the fifteenth. The dead maiden floating to Camelot on her barge is lovingly described. It is perhaps the single dominant image that caught the imagination of Victorian and Edwardian readers, from the Pre-Raphaelites to Anne of Green Gables.[39]

"The Holy Grail" of 1869 is narrated by Sir Percivale, who again joins Galahad, Percivale's sister the nun, Lancelot, Bors, and Gawaine on the quest inspired by the vision of the grail. The narrator Percivale is now a monk, speaking to his fellow monk Ambrosius. Tennyson rejects Lancelot's begetting of Galahad, again as an unworthy rumor.

Arthur is not present when the grail appears in his hall at Camelot, and opposes the quest for all except Galahad and the nun, the only true visionaries. He speaks for Tennyson before and after the quest, lamenting his knights' neglect of more immediate and more suitable duties in favor of this spiritual enthusiasm. Galahad alone achieves the spiritual city, though Percivale glimpses it. His temptation is provided by his first love, now a widow, who offers him the chance to marry her and become "an Arthur" to her people. Percivale flees; not even his fellow monk can entirely approve. Tennyson's portrait of Bors is affectionate; he, too, is offered a brief revelation while held prisoner among the pagans. They return to Arthur, a crumbling Camelot, and a diminished company of knights. Gawain has been enjoying himself among "merry maidens" in a pavilion. Last of all, Lancelot speaks of his hope to eradicate his one unspecified sin, his madness, displaced to this point in the story by Tennyson, and his experiences in the grail castle, altered only slightly from Malory. In his final speech Arthur reaffirms his original views on the destructive nature of the quest.

"Pelleas and Ettarre" (1869) and "The Last Tournament" (1871) provide Tennyson's most pessimistic vision of the decaying Round Table. Sir Pelleas's hopeless love for the sadistic Ettarde occurs early in Malory, and is resolved happily when Nynyve uses her magic powers to heal Pelleas and punish Ettarde. Tennyson accentuates the bitterness of an already cruel story, altering its ending. Further stung by Percivale's comment on Lancelot and Guinevere, Pelleas runs mad, denouncing Arthur and all his "ideals." In the "Last Tournament" he reappears as the Red Knight who sets up an anti–Round Table in mockery of Arthur. The other principal figures here are Tristram, newly married to Isolt of Brittany, and Arthur's fool Sir Dagonet. While Arthur rides off to fight the Red Knight and his heathen allies, Lancelot presides at the grim "Tournament of the Dead Innocence," whose prize is to be a ruby necklace obtained from a foundling infant girl discovered in an eagle's nest. The joust is disorderly, as is the court. While Lancelot and Guinevere are pained, the winner, Tristram, professes a cynical libertine philosophy to Dagonet, and rides off to his adulterous love, Isolt of Ireland. Like Gawain's, Tristram's character is blackened in Tennyson. Arthur wins an easy victory over the drunken Pelleas and burns his tower, Tristram returns to Isolt, who discusses the degenerative effect of Guinevere's sin on the Round Table and themselves. "The Last Tournament" ends with Mark's cowardly assassination of Tristram and Arthur's return to Camelot and a weeping Dagonet.

"Guinevere" (1859) replaces the meeting between Lancelot and Guinevere at her convent at Amesbury with a final confrontation between Arthur and Guinevere. The unsettling prattle of a "little novice" and Guinevere's own guilt-ridden reminiscence set the scene for Arthur's long culminating speech of judgment, farewell, and forgiveness. "Guinevere" remains easily the most controversial of the idylls. Its final image of the repentant Guinevere prostrate on the floor at the feet of her godlike husband offered Tennyson's readers a very different Guinevere from the decisive queen of Malory or William Morris's voluble character. George Bernard Shaw registered his disapproval of this scene's abasement of the female sex, which he felt could only be witnessed with satisfaction by the most complacent male audiences.[40] Still, perhaps Arthur is in greater peril than Guinevere; the queen's psychology, attractive or not, is effectively dramatized, while Arthur's dramatic speech offers unfortunate moments of self-pity and self-satisfaction that hardly make Tennyson's "blameless king" an appealing figure to the modern reader. Guinevere's belated realization that "she should have loved the highest" works well on a symbolic level, if less persuasively for us on a personal one. Whatever disagreements critics have expressed with Tennyson's decisions, the concept of a farewell scene for Arthur and Guinevere has been received with approval by subsequent readers, as its many imitators testify.[41]

Tennyson reworked his 1842 "Morte d'Arthur" into the "Passing of Arthur" in 1869. In its final version this last idyll describes Arthur's last battle with Mordred as well as its aftermath. Bedivere is represented as the bearer of this tradition, though he does not tell the story directly. Tennyson places the combat on the seacoast at midwinter. There is no attempt at any truce, but the drama of Arthur's duel with Mordred and Bedivere's disobedience follows Malory closely. The final speech and disappearance of Arthur in the barge with his three unidentified queens give an opportunity for some of the most celebrated lines in the *Idylls*. Tennyson ends optimistically with a hint of Arthur's triumphant reception somewhere beyond the dawn, with sunrise and the new year.

How does Tennyson's *Idylls of the King* stand up today as an Arthurian work? As English poetry pure and simple, Tennyson's *Idylls* is still recognized among the exceptional achievements of the nineteenth century. Whether it is ranked beside *In Memoriam* or just after it as Tennyson's masterwork depends on the taste of the critic. In Arthurian terms, the *Idylls* stands as one of the most important and least often acknowledged sources of modern Arthurian literature. In fact, Tennyson approaches more closely than any other English poet the elusive goal of the Arthurian epic.

Certain modern readers have found difficulties in appreciating Tennyson. Many of their problems arise from changes in historical perspective. Tennyson seems furthest from us in his "Dedication" and epilogue "To the Queen," extolling Prince Albert's Arthurian virtues and the greatness of the British Empire. His moral and symbolic reinterpretation of the Arthurian legends demands serious consideration. The *Idylls*'s stress on sexual morality and the sanctity of marriage and the family as prime civilizing factors in Arthur's code of chivalry should gain him as many admirers today among the new conservatives as it loses him elsewhere. The evocative descriptions in which Tennyson envisioned his magical city of Camelot and the bestiality of pre-Arthurian Britain unquestionably altered the way in which England and America still imagine the world of Arthur, through their own power and through the art and drama they inspired.

Perhaps the most influential of Tennyson's contributions to Arthurian literature is his reassertion of the central role of Arthur himself. In the *Idylls* Tennyson reclaims for King Arthur the dignity and importance of a principal character, no small feat after centuries of displacement into the background. During Tennyson's lifetime his critics objected that the Arthur of the *Idylls* was too good to be either true or likeable, and that Tennyson was trying to achieve the ultimate flattery of the Prince Regent. But despite a few unbearably priggish moments, Tennyson's Arthur does succeed. If we sympathize more deeply with Tennyson's sinners than with his occasionally cloying Arthurian saints, they too are part of Tennyson's achievement. A character vivid enough to be irritating is well worth celebration.

Varied reactions: the Pre-Raphaelites, Arnold, Wagner, and Twain. Viewed from close quarters, Tennyson's massive work tends to overshadow other nineteenth-century Arthurian compositions. Still, the late nineteenth century has established its reputation as a great age of Arthurian creativity not on account of one giant, but because of many artistic and literary works of great merit. While Tennyson was completing his *Idylls,* the painting and poetry of the Pre-Raphaelite movement, the revival of the Tristram legend by Matthew Arnold and Algernon Charles Swinburne, Wagner's operas and Mark Twain's satirical vision all revolutionized Arthuriana.

In 1849 Edward George Bulwer-Lytton (1803–73) published his attempt at an Arthurian epic, *King Arthur*.[42] His work continues in the tradition of Dryden, Blackmore, and Frere, reworking Arthurian material as contemporary political satire. Bulwer-Lytton complains of the same difficulties that had frustrated Dryden in the later seventeenth century: delays in the work's appearance would make many topical references unintelligible to later readers. This same problem stands between a twentieth-century public and Bulwer-Lytton's work. All the same, *King Arthur*'s largely original plot offers a number of highly entertaining episodes. Gawain's quest guided by a raven very like Poe's, ending in his capture by Vikings who intend to roast him as a sacrifice in support of "the greatest good of the greatest number" certainly deserves remembrance. Bulwer-Lytton's ingenious solution to the problem of Guinevere's adultery, splitting her into Geniveve, who marries Arthur, and Genevra, who marries Lancelot, may perhaps be better forgotten.

Matthew Arnold (1822–88) began to develop his "Tristram and Iseult" in 1849, and published the first version in 1852. Based in the main on a summary of the Tristram legend in Théodore de la Ville-marqué's 1841 *Revue de Paris* article on French Arthurian literature, Arnold's poem depicts Tristram on his deathbed in Brittany awaiting Iseult of Ireland's arrival. At his bedside sits Iseult of Brittany, his young wife. Arnold may well be reflecting on his early attraction to "Marguerite," the French girl he met briefly in Switzerland, and his marriage to Frances Lucy Wightman as he describes Tristram's relationship with his two Iseults.[43] In part 1 of the poem, Tristram's delirium allows him to relive his past, from the moment when he and Iseult of Ireland drink the love potion, through his exile, marriage to the other Iseult, and exploits with Arthur against the Romans. Arnold uses varied meters to represent a bard's narration, Tristram's speech, and, in part 2, Tristram's final dialogue with Iseult of Ireland. As these details indicate, Arnold innovates a good deal. Tristram and Iseult of Brittany now have children; in fact, the children are important figures in the poem. Tristram participates in Arthur's Roman wars here for the first time, and, for the first time, Iseult of Ireland arrives in time for an extended interview with her dying lover. The second half of part 2 describes Tristram and Iseult lying dead. Part 3, a year later, concerns Iseult of Brittany and her children, to whom she retells the story of Merlin and Vivien.

Arnold's special interest in Iseult of Brittany as a character is a distinctive feature of his poem. He sees her as a fragile and innocent victim of Tristram and Iseult's fatal passion. Her tale of Merlin and Vivien, with which the poem ends, may represent an oblique attempt on her part to understand the destructive attraction that bound her husband and her namesake. Arnold never explained in detail the connection between part 3 and the remainder of the poem; he remarked only that he added it to "relieve" the sadness of the poem's conclusion. On a structural level it is certainly necessary to balance Arnold's focus on Iseult of Brittany and her children in part 1: he could hardly abandon this group of characters after drawing our attention to them so pointedly. Does the seductive Vivien represent Iseult of Brittany's view of her rival, Iseult of Ireland? Is the child bride envious of Vivien's power? Arnold leaves any interpretation to his readers. His "Tristram and Iseult" is chronologically the first of the three major nineteenth-century Tristram narratives. It provides a far more sympathetic view of Tristram and his two Iseults than Tennyson does in "The Last Tournament." The rich descriptive detail of Arnold's work recreates a picturesque scene effectively. The dialogue of Tristram and Iseult is less successful, perhaps because of an unfortunate choice of meter.[44] Swinburne's 1882 *Tristram of Lyonesse* helped to revindicate further the Tristram story.

The rediscovery of Malory's *Morte Darthur* was one of the major inspirations of the group of writers and artists who formed the "Pre-Raphaelite Brotherhood" that was to disconcert the English cultural establishment of the mid–nineteenth century. William Morris (1834–96) and his friends Dante Gabriel Rossetti (1828–82) and Edward Burne-Jones (1833–98), principal members of the movement, all contributed to Arthurian art in different ways, Burne-Jones and Rossetti through their paintings of scenes from the legend, Morris through art and poetry. It seems significant that the pioneering group project of the trio, their ill-fated Oxford Union murals of 1857–59, should be based on Malory.[45] While the technical inexperience of the collaborators led to the rapid deterioration of this early work, their later experiments were much more successful. The Pre-Raphaelites aspired to return to the aesthetic principles of medieval and early Renaissance art. Their interest in craftsmanship and design found outlets in Morris's companies, producing innovative furniture, tapestries, textiles, and stained glass, as well as in their paintings and illustrations.[46] While the art history of the Pre-Raphaelite movement extends beyond the scope of this book, it is important to recognize the interdependence of Arthurian art and literature, particularly when considering a writer like William Morris who was also a painter.

Morris's 1858 *The Defence of Guenevere and Other Poems* is best known today for its title work, "The Defence of Guenevere," though the volume also contained five other Arthurian poems. The poet's daughter, May Morris, also printed several Arthurian fragments in her edition of Morris's works, and states that her father "had certainly designed a complete Arthurian cycle."[47] The "Defence of Guenevere" takes place at the moment when Guinevere is standing trial for adultery before the assembled knights, just before Lancelot appears to rescue her. Guinevere speaks in her own defense, addressing "Gauwaine," her principal accuser. Her speech is hardly a reasoned argument; Morris's poem studies a proud, defiant, and tormented Pre-Raphaelite beauty as the queen reflects on the tragic history of her love for Lancelot. In its use of color, light, and stylized gesture, the "Defence of Guenevere" might be read as a verbal depiction of a Pre-Raphaelite painting. Guinevere herself is imagined as a distinctively Pre-Raphaelite beauty, with her mass of long wavy hair; long neck, eyes, and fingers; full lips; and broad forehead. The sensual gorgeousness of the poem and its emotional intensity lend it great power. For the first time since Malory, Guinevere is given an effective voice.

Morris is less successful in his other Arthurian poems. "King Arthur's Tomb" reworks the final meeting of Lancelot and Guinevere, now set at Arthur's sepulchre. Still impassioned lovers, they are parted by Guinevere's new sense of guilt. In "Sir Galahad: A Christmas Mystery," Galahad begins by regretting his chastity, and then is rewarded by a vision of Christ and the presence of the grail. "The Chapel in Lyoness," written in the form of a play, dramatizes the agonizing death of Sir Ozanna le cure Hardy, consoled by Galahad and Bors. "A Good Knight in Prison" narrates Lancelot's rescue of Sir Guy from a pagan castle. "Near Avalon" describes a mysterious ship carrying six ladies and six knights; once again Guinevere and not Arthur is Morris's concern. The sails bear her image, and the yellow hair the knights carry in their helmets may also be hers, possibly a reminiscence of Giraldus Cambrensis. These minor Arthurian poems bear witness to Morris's inventiveness; many of the scenes he describes seem to be his own variations on Malory.

The many famous Arthurian paintings and illustrations of Morris, Burne-Jones, and Rossetti offer an instructive visual correlative to Morris's Arthurian poems. Although the faded Oxford Union murals can only be reconstructed academically, many other works survive in excellent condition. William Morris's portrait of his wife Jane as Queen Guinevere is only the best known of many Arthurian designs for which he was responsible. Rossetti's illustrations of Tennyson translate the *Idylls of the King* into Pre-Raphaelite terms. Burne-Jones's paintings of Merlin and Nimue, and of the dying Arthur give the legend an opulent and sensuous presence. The innovative combination of words and images that the Pre-Raphaelites created lent the Arthurian world a renewed mystery, glamour, and passion, to the disquiet of their more conservative contemporaries.[48]

A new Continental influence on English and American Arthurian works made itself felt for the first time in the 1850s. Richard Wagner's operas have been accepted in the standard repertory for so long that it may perhaps be useful to recall the furor they caused on their first appearance. None is Arthurian in the strictest sense of the word, since Wagner divorced both the grail and Tristan stories from any Arthurian associations he found in his medieval sources. *Lohengrin* (1850) and *Parsifal* (1882) pick up Wolfram von Eschenbach's concept of the order of grail knights. Lohengrin, Parsifal's son, is sent to defend Elsa of Brabant in a judicial duel. *Parsifal* is Wagner's reworking of Wolfram's *Parzifal,* retaining Parzifal's character as the innocent "Fool," and the crucial test question that the Fool fails and then answers, but omitting Parzifal's love story and the adventures of Gawain. *Tristan und Isolde* (1865) cuts through many of the complications of that story by eliminating or obscuring Isolde's marriage to Marke and Tristan's to Isolde of Brittany. The opera centers on the doomed lovers' journey toward death, as death is inextricably bound up in their exalted love. Wagner's librettos, which he wrote himself, give expression to his new dramatic aspirations for the opera. In the process, his unified music-dramas with their spectacular sets and thematically integrated music enhanced the mystery and passion of the legends he chose. The impact of Wagner's theory and practice can be traced in the criticism of the later nineteenth century, and especially in the dramatic and operatic works of his imitators, many of them Arthurian.[49]

The most elaborate nineteenth-century treatment of the Tristram story in English is Algernon Swinburne's 1882 *Tristram of Lyonesse,* a full-length account of the legend in iambic pentameter couplets, based on a combination of Malory and the French romances.[50] *Tristram of Lyonesse* belongs in the Pre-Raphaelite camp. Swinburne returns many of the features that Tennyson had softened or eliminated from his history of Arthur. On their voyage to Cornwall Tristram and Isolde discuss Morgause's affairs with Arthur and Lamoracke. Malory's more attractive

Nynyve replaces Tennyson's Vivien once more and rescues Pelleas from
Ettarde. In his conclusion Swinburne retains the black-and-white sails
and the treachery of Isolde of Brittany, rather than Mark's assassination
of Tristram. Swinburne's heavy use of alliteration, assonance, and in-
cantatory rhythms have made his work very much an acquired taste.
His sensuous retelling of the Tristram story, like much of Swinburne's
work, seems to be directed toward a rather select audience.

Swinburne returned to Malory in 1896 for "The Tale of Balen,"
about Malory's Balin, in nine-line stanzas. A somewhat disappointing
attempt, it seems less inspired than *Tristram of Lyonesse*. Perhaps the
spare tragedy of the two brother knights simply did not lend itself to
Swinburne's ornate versification.

Reminiscent of Swinburne in a number of ways are Aubrey Beardsley's
illustrations for Malory's *Morte Darthur,* first printed by Dent in 1886.[51]
These stylized black-and-white art nouveau drawings were, in some
cases, highly controversial, like much of Beardsley's work. They combine
the appearance of a medieval manuscript page, with ornate borders and
initials, and a new hard-edged, abstracted form. The medieval influence
connects Beardsley with the Pre-Raphaelites, especially with the publications of Morris's Kelmscott press. The outrageousness and sexual
ambiguities of Beardsley's work are entirely his own, however.

American literature makes its first distinguished contribution to the
Arthurian legend with Mark Twain's *A Connecticut Yankee in King
Arthur's Court* (1889).[52] It had been sixty years since Thomas Love
Peacock explored the potential of Arthurian literature as a vehicle for
social satire. Twain's extraordinary comic ingenuity carries the joke a
great deal further. The return of Arthur, Merlin, and other characters
for a modern event was a commonplace of Arthurian drama, if not of
other genres of Arthurian literature. Twain's novel brings a nineteenth-
century American back in time to meet the knights of the Round Table
on their own ground. It is the first major Arthurian work to take this
approach, now a standard procedure for many twentieth-century Arthurian writers. Merlin is under fire from the start, though Arthur and
Lancelot remain more or less positive figures. Twain's attack on the
nineteenth-century idealization of the Middle Ages may have been fueled
by his disapproval of the ill-fated Southern cult of chivalry. His satire
of the narrator, the Connecticut Yankee himself, has been less obvious
to many readers. "Sir Boss" 's free expression of his own intellectual
superiority as a man of the present, "a giant among pygmies," his
commercial rapacity, and his lavish demonstration of the mass destruction

of postchivalric warfare demonstrate Twain's intent beyond doubt. The fact that this feature of the book is so often missed may speak for the pertinence of Twain's satire, as well as for its readers' continuing complacency.

The late nineteenth century's preoccupation with the revival of King Arthur extended well beyond these few major works. After the tentative experiments of the English Renaissance and Restoration, and the hesitations of the mid–nineteenth century, the onrush of Arthurian works after 1850 seems almost overpowering. Arthur emerges from the Victorian era, no longer as an obscure topic with little contemporary appeal, but once again as a major theme of English literature. Twain's novel might be seen as a presage of the fact that American writers, too, would have something to say about King Arthur. When in 1895 the London Lyceum company commissioned an Arthurian play from J. Comyns Carr, with sets by Burne-Jones, music by Sir Arthur Sullivan, and Henry Irving and Ellen Terry in the leading roles, they bore witness to the strong artistic and commercial interest the legends still enjoyed at the end of the century. Comyns Carr's play also looks forward to the active Arthurian drama of the future but warns future playwrights of the difficulties inherent in such a project.[53] On these foundations, twentieth–century authors built still more ambitious visions of Camelot.

Chapter Five

Arthurian Literature of the Twentieth Century

Threading a path through the jungle of luxuriant twentieth-century Arthurian literature is a full-time occupation in itself. Fortunately, a number of useful studies cover this period in detail, for example those of Nathan C. Starr, Raymond Thompson, and Brewer and Taylor, as well as relevant entries in the *Arthurian Encyclopedia*.[1] These works cover the material discussed in this chapter in much greater detail than here. The vitality and diversity of new Arthurian works produced during this century is startling. To understand them properly, continuities as well as changes need to be stressed.

In many respects, the Arthurian literature of the early twentieth century continues trends already developing in the nineteenth. Arthurian narrative poetry in the tradition of Tennyson and the Pre-Raphaelites still flourished, and the theater bore witness to the continuing appeal of *Tristan und Isolde*. Malory remained a primary source for basic Arthurian history, with attempts to draw in early Celtic texts also apparent.

One feature of twentieth-century English and American literature in general with special importance for the study of King Arthur, is the widening division between popular and "serious" literature. This gap was actually developing in the later nineteenth century. Before then, major authors were not necessarily adverse to mass audiences, and as late as the mid–nineteenth century Dickens and Tennyson were both popular writers. Some works have always been written for rarefied and exclusive circles, but audiences with varying degrees of sophistication could enjoy *Sir Gawain and the Green Knight* or the *Morte Darthur*. Perhaps the increasing specialization of the publishing industry or the isolation of literary elites account for the situation readers experience today, in which two literatures challenge them with very different intellectual demands. The Arthurian legend's ability to cross barriers of genre and stylistic level is demonstrated by the works to be discussed in this chapter, with range from the most hermetic modern poetry to the comic book.

A second major force altering the Arthurian literature of the twentieth century is that of Arthurian studies themselves. New theories of the real significance of the Arthurian legend, archaeology, anthropology, and historical studies have all been employed in literature, the better to recreate the King Arthur's world. Perhaps no other subject better illustrates the interplay of scholarship and the arts.

A chronological survey of the most characteristic twentieth-century Arthurian literature brings out the principal features of this expanding body of work. Twentieth-century crises of faith, interest in the occult, the rise of genre fiction, feminism, and contemporary political comment all find their place in modern Arthuriana. Our own era's portraits of King Arthur mirror our own faces.

Arthurian Literature to 1930

For the first three decades of the twentieth century, Arthurian literature remained largely a domain of poets, with plays in verse and paintings or illustrations of the legends second in popularity. Early twentieth-century Arthurian works alternate between the accessible and the difficult, displaying the wild stylistic diversity appropriate to literature in a dynamic state.

Edwin Arlington Robinson. The American poet Edwin Arlington Robinson (1869–1935) is best known today for his shorter poems, "Miniver Cheevy," "Richard Cory," and "Mr. Flood's Party," all ubiquitous in anthologies. His three substantial Arthurian narrative poems are comparatively unknown. *Merlin* was first published in 1917, *Lancelot* in 1920, and *Tristram* in 1927.[2] All three poems are written in blank verse, and adhere to the unexpurgated Malory's basic account of the fall of the Round Table.

Among Robinson's innovations should be listed his conception of Merlin's "imprisonment" in Brittany as a period of voluntary retirement to sybaritic pleasure with Vivian; he returns to Camelot twice, although he recognizes that he cannot change Arthur's fate. On the second visit, Merlin does not even meet Arthur, who is setting out to make war on Lancelot. The more positive treatment of Vivian's relationship with Merlin recalls Pre-Raphaelite art, Burne-Jones's paintings of the "Beguiling of Merlin" in particular, a great deal more than it does Malory or Tennyson. Merlin's visionary search for "a nameless light" (295) does suggest Tennyson's "Merlin and the Gleam," even as his comments that Merlin is somehow outside ordinary time, "my memories go forward" (287) anticipates T. H. White's much more famous Merlyn "living backward."

Lancelot keeps Tennyson's frivolous Gawain and attempts to combine him with Malory's concept of him as a vengeful brother. The story begins before Lancelot and Guinevere are entrapped, and ends after their last parting. Made up largely of dialogues and meditations, the poem has received critical recognition for Arthur's frantic speech as he waits for the news of Guinevere's execution.[3] Robinson's handling of Gawain's new deathbed conversation with Lancelot and the meeting of Lancelot and Guinevere at Amesbury is less satisfactory.

Like Matthew Arnold, Robinson develops the character of Isolt of the White Hands in his *Tristram,* evidently also attracted by the pathos of the child bride observing the fatal passion of Tristram and Isolt the Fair. Her role is all the more peripheral in Robinson because Tristram does not even die in Brittany, but returns to Cornwall to be assassinated by King Mark's satellite Andred. *Tristram*'s fourth notable female character is Morgan le Fay, whose determined pursuit of Tristram begins at the Irish Isolt's wedding with King Mark. Robinson's Tristram never becomes the libertine that Tennyson made him; he remains an obsessed lover for whom death provides a merciful release.

Any writer daring enough to take up the subject of Arthur in blank verse challenges direct comparison with Tennyson, not to mention Morris and Swinburne. In spite of his more contemporary language, Robinson's verse is less interesting than theirs, and often diffuse, largely because of his weakness for long, meditative speeches. His new Arthurian situations do interest the student of the history of the legend. It would be going too far to interpret Robinson's problems as a sign that Arthurian narrative poetry was a dying literary form. His attempt does suggest, though, that it would require an extraordinary performance to extend this main avenue of Arthurian literature much past the *Idylls of the King.*

James Branch Cabell, *Jurgen: A Comedy of Justice* **(1919).** To approximately the same decades as Edwin Arlington Robinson's works belongs James Branch Cabell's controversial novel, *Jurgen,* which first appeared in 1919, and was rereleased in 1922 after battling obscenity charges.[4] Among its pawnbroker hero's many amatory adventures, one Arthurian incident involves him in a love affair with the young Guinevere, aided surprisingly by that heroine's father. This American narrative offers an antichivalric view of the Arthurian world that takes off from the tradition of Twain in a new direction.

T. S. Eliot, *The Waste Land* **(1922).** Thomas Stearns Eliot's *Waste Land,* first published in 1922, is still celebrated as a major landmark in twentieth-century poetry. As Arthurian or un-Arthurian in its own way as Spenser's *Faerie Queene, The Waste Land* is fundamental for students of the Arthurian legends as a modern reinterpretation of the grail story. Eliot referred to Jessie L. Weston's book in the grail, *From Ritual to Romance* (1920), as one source for the plan and symbolism of the poem. *From Ritual to Romance* develops the pioneering work of Sir James G. Frazier's *Golden Bough,* interpreting the myth of the grail as a reflection of primitive fertility rituals. *The Waste Land* may stand as a primary instance of the relationship between new directions in Arthurian scholarship and innovative Arthurian literature.[5]

Eliot uses Weston's theory to transmute the land rendered barren by the impotence of the Fisher King into an emblem of the sterility of modern existence. The Fisher King himself, or his modern equivalent, speaks in section 3, "The Fire Sermon," and asks toward the end of section 5, "What the Thunder Said," "Shall I at least set my lands in order?" The "waste land" itself recurs throughout the poem, whether as a rocky and waterless desert, or in the barren cosmopolitan encounters of the city, usually London. The Tristan legend also contributes to Eliot's work, through Wagner's *Tristan and Isolde;* Eliot quotes from the Irish sailor's song at the opening of act 1, and from act 3 when the dying Tristan is told that Isolde's ship is not yet visible. Both quotations express longing, as the inhabitants of the Waste Land yearn for release, and for real feeling. Other images like the ruined chapel of section 5, or the ambiguous sea throughout the poem, can also be linked with the legends of the quest of the Holy Grail.

The Waste Land make no reference to Arthur himself. As in Wagner, the Tristan legend and the grail are divested of their Arthurian connections. Nevertheless, Eliot's work may remain the most memorable use of any Arthurian motif in modern English or American poetry. Mentioning no names, Eliot still gives the Fisher King and his ravaged kingdom an abstract, universal application that they cannot attain as Amfortas or Logres.

Thomas Hardy, *The Famous Tragedy of Isolde, Queen of Cornwall at Tintagel in Lyonnesse* **(1923).** With Thomas Hardy (1840–1928) the theatrical vogue of the Tristan legend entered a new phase. That grand old man of English letters, already established as a powerful novelist of rural tragedy centered in the Wessex countryside, and respected as a poet, published his "mummer's play," *The Famous Tragedy of the Queen of Cornwall at Tintagel in Lyonnesse,* in 1923. He described it as a mummer's play, and it was first performed by an amateur troup from Dorchester. In his one-act account of Tristram's end, Hardy unleashes the latent violence of Isolde of Ireland's character, glimpsed on occasion in her medieval legends. After meeting and intimidating her Breton rival, Hardy's Isolde is given her first opportunity to avenge Tristram's assassination by killing her husband, King Mark. She then hurls herself over a cliff, employing one of Hardy's favorite modes of suicide. This compact play focuses on the marital tensions between the two Isoldes, Tristram, and Mark, perhaps recalling marital tensions in the Hardy household. It is well described in Brewer and Taylor as a spare, realistic drama that cuts away the romantic images of Wagner and Swinburne to focus on the legend as a bitter domestic tragedy.[6]

John Masefield. John Masefield (1874–1967), appointed Poet Laureate in 1930, returned to the Arthurian legends repeatedly throughout his career as poet and novelist. Masefield is most often recalled today for a few of his sea lyrics, founded on his service as a merchant seaman. His Arthurian poems include *Tristan and Isolt: A Play in Verse* (1927); *Midsummer Night, A Verse Cycle* (1928); "The Love Gift" and "Tristan's Singing," in *Minnie Maylow's Story and other Tales and Scenes* (1931); "The Ballad of Sir Bors," in *Collected Poems* (1932); and "Tristan and Isolt," in *On the Hill* (1949). Masefield uses many uncommon Welsh sources, in particular the triads and the "Spoils of Annwyn."

Arthur also appear in a number of Masefield's prose works. *Badon Parchments* (1947) uses an epistolary narrative centered around the battle of Mount Badon as an occasion for political comment on World War II. His Count Artorios makes an interesting brief appearance in *Basilissa* (1940), Masefield's historical novel about the empress Theodora, as a British nobleman requesting foreign aid from Byzantium.[7]

Masefield's most entrancing and influential contributions to twentieth-century Arthurian literature are made through his fantasies for children, in particular *The Midnight Folk* (1927) and *The Box of Delights* (1935).[8] Their irresistible amalgam of pirates, witches, English country life, and poetry has never been matched in juvenile fiction. It is regrettable that much distinguished children's literature, frequently of higher quality than a good deal of critically acclaimed adult fiction, is ignored by students of literature. In the case of Masefield, its status as children's literature has led critics to neglect what may be that prolific author's best work, his most original depiction of the court of King Arthur, and a primary source of T. H. White's *Sword in the Stone.* More than one authoritative source tells us that White was a particularly enthusiastic reader of *The Midnight Folk.*[9] In that work and in *The Box of Delights* White would have enjoyed among other features the schoolboy hero Kay's adventures among the animals. In *The Midnight Folk* a "suit of wings" allows him to fly with the Bat and an otter skin lets him swim with Tom Otter. In *The Box of Delights* the magic of Herne the Hunter transforms Kay successively to a young deer, a wild duck, and a fish as they elude Kay's pursuers in the form of wolves, hawks, and a pike. The young Arthur's animal transformation in *The Sword in the Stone* are more explicitly didactic—White was, after all, a former school-master—but they draw much of their sheer delight from Masefield's.

Where in *Basilissa* (ll. 129–53) Masefield describes a historical Arthur of the early sixth century, in *The Midnight Folk* (183–91) Masefield presents his most attractive picture of Arthur's legendary court. Young Kay is given a miniature Arthurian adventure when he is summoned from his bed to Arthur's camp. On the way, he meets the Black Knight at the ford, and, in the manner of the more flamboyant chivalric romances, chops his head off at one blow. King Arthur's court has magically reappeared; his guide Lancelot tells Kay, "Now we are remaking what we undid." The most vivid descriptions in the lively scene at Arthur's camp are of Queen Guinevere, "a somewhat fierce-looking and splendid beauty," driving her chariot, and of Merlin. "He had a strange, troubled, happy face, as though he were always having very difficult puzzles set to him and always finding the answers" (191). Arthur sends three of his knights to help find the treasure that Kay and his friends are looking for. Kay awakens just as he is about to speak to the king himself, but the experience is not dismissed altogether as a dream; King Arthur's knights do in fact help to recover the lost treasure. *The Midnight Folk*'s Arthur combines generalized Arthurian place-name lore, as in "Arthur's Camp" or "King Arthur's Ride," the legend of Arthur's return, and the image of Arthur as a kind of Oberon. A later Arthurian grace-note puts "The Beginner's Merlin," "Merlin's 100 Best Bewitchals," and "Shape-Changing for all, by M. le Fay" on the bookself of Kay's governess, the witch Sylvia Daisy Pouncer. Masefield's happy reworking of Arthurian material tantalizes its readers with its brevity. T. H. White picked up many of these threads in

1937–38, when he wrote *The Sword in the Stone,* but he did not recapture Masefield's light touch or kaleidoscopic powers of invention.

The Thirties: Charles Williams and T. H. White

Some of the most influential Arthurian literature of the twentieth century dates from the 1930s. To this period belongs the rise into prominence of the serious Arthurian novel. While nineteenth-century authors had begun to explore the possibilities of Arthurian prose fiction, prose was hardly the dominant medium for narratives of King Arthur in the age of Tennyson and the Pre-Raphaelites. It remained for writers of the 1930s to acclimate Arthurian themes to the novel. Mystical spirituality and popularization stretch the legends of Arthur in opposite directions throughout this period. King Arthur emerges from this key decade as the monarch of a vastly extended realm.

Charles Williams and his circle. With Charles Williams (1886–1945) the Arthurian legend enters what might be described as a twentieth-century "metaphysical" phase. The novels of C. S. Lewis and John Cowper Powys also travel down this path, as the original *Queste del Saint Graal,* Spenser, Tennyson, and Eliot had done for shorter distances before them. Williams survives in English literary history as a member of the Oxford "Inklings" circle, together with C. S. Lewis and J. R. R. Tolkien. Williams shares with his Oxford contemporaries and followers their interest in myth, medieval literature, and Anglican theology, occasionally recalling the nineteenth-century "muscular Christianity" of Charles Kingsley. These three interests reappear to varying degrees in the academic and creative work of each member of the group. Of the "Inklings" circle, Williams unquestionably made the most important contribution to the history of Arthurian literature. He is also, unfortunately, the least accessible writer.

Some critics, notably Brewer and Taylor, blame a recent lack of interest in religious poetry for Williams's failure to find a large modern audience, together with his deliberately hermetic style.[10] These certainly seem to be important limiting factors. Williams's impenetrability seems to be rooted in the nature of his endeavor, and in the specific character of his poetry and spirituality. Like William Butler Yeats, to whom he has been somewhat unjustly compared, Williams reworks traditional legends and figures into a complex personal mythology and theology. In Williams's system, Arthurian history is centered around the grail quest, that legend now being used to symbolize the alienation of the created world from God. Williams developed his allegorization of Arthur chiefly in two volumes of poetry, *Taliesin through Logres* (1938) and *The Region of the Summer Stars* (1944). *Arthurian Torso* (1948) contains an unfinished history of Arthurian literature by Williams himself, and a commentary on Williams's cycle of Arthurian poems by his friend C. S. Lewis. More recent detailed analyses of Williams's poetry appear in Brewer and Taylor and in a number of articles by Karl Heinz Göller. They commend in particular Williams's injection of spirituality into Arthurian writing, and, on the technical side, the vigor and energy of his verse, modeled to some degree on that of Gerard Manley Hopkins.[11]

It is not the mere fact that Williams is a religious poet, nor the realization that he is a difficult one that has denied him a sizeable public. Williams's work is intellectually exclusive, much more so than T. S. Eliot's. His Christianity, like that of Lewis, is a decisive and uncompromising creed, not perhaps totally appealing to all Christians. Meanwhile, the jarring rhythms of the verse itself discourage the reader's approach. Like Milton, Williams has achieved his "fit audience, though few": his vision remains accessible to specialists and a select company of devotees, thanks to the detailed commentaries of his diligent glossators. But, as C. S. Lewis himself pointed out, Williams's work focuses on a small group of the visionary elect among Arthur's knights, paralleling the elect he drew to himself in his lifetime and after.

Williams uses Malory's account of Arthurian history, but employs the events of the legend to represent a "higher reality." For instance, Byzantium is equated with creation, or with unfallen humanity (246). Nimue is nature, Merlin's mother. Camelot become the City of God. Elaine's substitution for Guinevere when Galahad is conceived parallels the substitution of Christ for sinful humanity in the Crucifixion. Galahad and Taliesin, Arthur's poet, are the central figures of Williams's cycle of poems. The influence of Tennyson is still visible in the threat of passion against divine order. Guinevere's failure to fulfill her proper function as Arthur's queen is here condemned on a mystical plane, though in Williams Arthur fails reprehensibly too, through his incest. The symbolic role of Queen Guinevere as matter, or as the sensuous element in the universe, perhaps wears thinnest for the modern female reader.[12]

Williams also wrote a grail novel, *The War in Heaven* (1930), set in the twentieth century, in which good and evil characters struggle for possession of the Holy Grail.[13] It provides aspiring readers of Williams's Arthuriad with a good introduction to his ideas. Neither in his poetry nor in his novel is Williams much interested in characterization. This lack of concern for individual personages for their own sakes further distances his audiences from engagement in his works, though it un-questionably aids Williams's presentation of universal concepts.

C. S. Lewis's novel *That Hideous Strength* (1945), completes his "Space," or *Perelandra* trilogy.[14] His hero, Ransom, "Mr. Fisher King," succeeds Arthur as the twentieth-century leader of Logres. His enemy is N.I.C.E., the "National Institute of Coordinated Experiments," which plans to exhume Merlin in order to use his magic in its program of genetic engineering and mind control. The weaknesses of *That Hideous Strength* tend to lie in its curious juxtaposition of Christian moral instruction, gore, and, again, a rather Tennysonian view of Jane, his Guinevere figure, as a rebellious wife. Lewis's academic experiences at Oxford and Cambridge enable him to bring the corrupt intellectual community of N.I.C.E. to life with satirical zest that may be the most successful feature of the book.

J. R. R. Tolkien's contributions to Arthurian literature and scholarship extend over a longer period, but may prove ultimately to carry the greatest impact. His medieval scholarship is most familiar to modern Arthurians from his work as an editor and translator of *Sir Gawain and the Green Knight*.[15] While his fantasies, *The Hobbit*, and the trilogy *The Lord of the Rings*, are not ostensibly Arthurian, they contain some familiar motifs: his handling of the king Aragorn and his wizard advisor, Gandalf, may owe the most to King Arthur. The proliferation of triologies of Arthurian fantasy novels in the 1970s, following hard on the enormous popularity of Tolkien's trilogy in the 1960s, perhaps offers the most striking testimony to Tolkien's importance for modern Arthurian literature.

John Cowper Powys and the rise of the Arthurian novel.   John Cowper Powys's *Glastonbury Romance* (1932) is a massive grail fantasy. His other Arthurian novel, *Porius* (1951), falls into the category of historical fiction; it is a study of a sixth-century Briton's decision to join Arthur as a "distant mirror" of the twentieth century.[16] *A Glastonbury Romance* takes place in twentieth-century Glastonbury, where characters with clashing ideologies compete to exploit the many legendary sites of the area. The grail itself is a spiritual entity whose power is sought throughout the novel as its characters reenact many Arthurian scenes. Behind Powys's novel lies a dualistic metaphysical vision in which good and evil aspects of an eternal "first cause" are eternally at war. Powys explores problems of suffering, sadomasochism, and psychic powers. In this connection, his two unusual Merlins are notable.

Arthurian legends also play a role in John Steinbeck's *Tortilla Flat* (1935), at least according to Steinbeck himself.[17] A lifelong admirer of Malory, he explains the group of California friends gathered at Danny's house in his novel as a new Round Table. Critics disagree about the strength of the connection. Steinbeck's most direct contribution to Arthurian literature was not to appear until the 1970s.

James Joyce used the Tristan legend in 1939 in *Finnegans Wake* to channel the fantasy life of H. C. Earwicker, the middle-aged pub-keeper who dreams of himself as Tristran and his daughter Isabel as Isolde.[18] Here knowledge of the original legend is helpful for understanding the workings of Earwicker's inventive mind.

T. H. White. The best-known Arthurian work of the twentieth century is arguably Terence Hanbury White's series of Arthurian novels, *The Once and Future King*, begun in 1937 and completed in 1958.[19] Like its principal source, Malory's *Morte Darthur* and Tennyson's *Idylls of the King*, White's reworking of Arthurian material exerted an impressive influence on later compositions. It was the direct source of two popular dramatizations, Walt Disney's animated *The Sword in the Stone* and Lerner and Loewe's musical *Camelot*. White's conceptions of Arthurian characters, and his use of anachronistic humor have also infiltrated the literature of a surprising number of his successors, so that disentangling Malory from White becomes a serious problem for the unexperienced reader.

A Cambridge undergraduate essay on Malory, whom White regarded as the greatest writer in English after Shakespeare, seems to have sparked White's "preface to Malory," *The Sword in the Stone*, published in 1938.[20] White's account of the young Arthur, "the Wart," and his tutor Merlin also betrays White's fondness for Masefield's fantasies more in the first than in the 1958 revised version. Even the striking notion of Merlin as tutor to the boy Arthur may owe something to Masefield's Kay, suffering with a witch for a governess. Nevertheless, this is perhaps the most original section of *The Once and Future King*. Its affectionate and anachronistic spoof of Sir Ector, King Pellinor, and Sir Grummore Grummoreson as English sportin' gentlemen is an exuberant burlesque. English education, which White had experienced painfully from both sides of the desk, comes in for some lively satire as well.

In his second volume, published in 1939–40 as *The Queen of Air and Darkness,* and later reissued as *The Witch in the Wood,* White's strong autobiographical impulses led him into greater difficulties. He attempted to exorcise his antipathy for his mother by depicting her in the person of Queen Morgause, whom we first meet engaged in the loveable occupation of boiling a live cat. The intensity of his personal feelings tend to interfere with artistic control here, as they do to a less distressing extent later in White's identification of himself with Lancelot, the hero of his next Arthurian novel, *The Ill-made Knight* (1940–41). White explains what he sees as Lancelot's sense of inferiority in Malory by making him ugly, an interesting authorial decision that tends to divide his audience sharply into admirers and critics, and perhaps also into romantics and realists.[21]

With the conclusion of *The Once and Future King*, White got into difficulties again. As it appeared in 1958, *The Once and Future King* ended with *The Candle in the Wind*, which had originally been outlined as a play before being written as a novel.[22] At its conclusion, Arthur, about to face Mordred's cannon in his last battle, sends young "Tom of Warwick," the young Thomas Malory, away to pass on the story of the Round Table to posterity. White's concerns about World War II and longing for the elimination of warfare led him to add a fifth volume, *The Book of Merlyn*, which brings Arthur back to Merlyn and the animals he met as a boy for an investigation of human aggressiveness. This didactic and political conclusion came as a shock to White's publishers when it was submitted as the final book of the series. As a result of their disagreement, *The Book of Merlyn* was not published until 1977, thirteen years after White's death.[23] Two scenes from *Merlyn*, depicting Arthur's experiences among the ants and the wild geese, were salvaged from the rejected book and inserted in the rewritten *Sword in the Stone*. White's final book is misanthropic, pontifical, and in deadly earnest. Its most appealing feature is the opportunity to encounter White's characters again, and its main pitfall is a tendency to lecture. As White's biographer Sylvia Townsend Warner points out, probably the most important feature to note here is White's new version of Malory's conclusion, in which Arthur, Lancelot, and Guinevere all reach their final destinations at last.[24]

White follows Malory for his basic narrative, at times translating word for word from the fifteenth-century text, at other times expanding and explaining it in great detail. This procedure can confuse many unwary readers into crediting White with a good deal of Malory. It must be admitted that, for an imaginative reader of the *Morte Darthur*, the explanations and expansions do not always add anything useful or necessary to the story. At his best, White is a marvelously entertaining storyteller. Schoolboy humor is an occasional distraction; sometimes the slapstick fun runs out of control and persists too long for anyone's enjoyment. White is at his worst when he is expounding a political theory or when coping with major female characters. Guinevere, the great problem figure of Arthurian literature, comes off better than Morgause, certainly, but she never altogether captures White's understanding or compassion in the way Arthur, Merlyn, and Lancelot do.

The Once and Future King has unquestionably altered our vision of the Arthurian world. Its concept of the absentminded magician Merlyn, who "lives backward" drew on Malory's mischievous wizard with the penchant for disguises in a new way. The idea of Merlyn's education of Arthur has continued to fascinate writers as different in character as Thomas Berger and Mary Stewart. Malory's code of chivalry is simplified drastically as White's Arthur urges his knights to reject the idea of "Might is Right" in favor of "Might in the Service of Right," perhaps enhancing its appeal for modern audiences. The heavy ironies White employs have certainly been much appreciated by an age that particularly relishes that form of wit.

White saw the Arthurian legend as a Greek tragedy of retribution, with the "Orkney clan" exacting revenge on Arthur for his father's adultery with Igerne, as well as for his own inadvertent incest with Morgause. This vision finds an interesting forerunner in the sixteenth-century *Misfortunes of Arthur*. Where the play attempted to elevate the legendary characters to heights of Senecan magniloquence, White deflates them, charmingly for the most part. In the movement from innocent hope to cruel disillusionment that characterizes Arthur's story, White keeps his personages' feet on the ground. His version of the Arthurian legend has won its wide popularity through its readable prose, anachronistic comedy, and endearing pathos. Where Williams tried to heighten Arthur's legend to a mystical level, White endeavored to make it accessible as a story to the twentieth-century common reader. The success of these two very different but approximately contemporary endeavors illustrates the multiple vision with which this century's writers have seen Arthur.

As a footnote to T. H. White, it may be useful to mention here the two successful dramatizations of this work, which extended the fame and influence of *The Once and Future King* still further. Alan J. Lerner and Frederick Loewe's musical *Camelot* (1960; film 1967) has been criticized for diminishing White's concept of Arthur.[25] White himself does not seem to have objected greatly, at least according to Sylvia Townsend Warner. The compression of the story natural to the drama is of course intensified by the need to insert songs at regular intervals. *Camelot*'s attempt to depict White's childlike Arthur does cross the line into idiocy on more than one occasion, unless the role is played very carefully indeed. Lancelot is no longer ugly nor middle-aged, though White's insistence on his chastity before his shocking experience with Elaine the Fair may have contributed to his appearance in the musical as a rather smug young Galahad figure, an irritating interpretation that John Boorman's film *Excalibur* (1981) also endorses. *Camelot* is perhaps most famous today for its opening description of Arthur's ideal kingdom, as much Tennyson as White, which was to become associated with the administration of John F. Kennedy.

Walt Disney released an animated film of White's *Sword in the Stone* in 1963, a lively and charming adaptation of the narrative that translates White's individual brand of comedy into a highly compatible medium.[26] After Hollywood's intermittent struggles to inch some remotely Arthurian narrative past the censors in the 1950s, White gave Arthurian drama a new impetus.

After T. H. White: The Arthurian Explosion, 1970–86

The ubiquity of Arthurian references in recent twentieth-century literature can induce paranoia in their chroniclers; the temptation to reduce criticism to an annotated bibliography becomes extreme. Arthur has invaded every rank of literature, from the most abstruse modern poetry to the comic strip. Interest in his legend has probably never been so great since the thirteenth century. In terms of quantity the 1970s and '80s in particular have witnessed an explosion of Arthurian works. In terms of quality, less can be said.

At least some of the credit for this new wave of interest in Arthur should go to T. H. White. By making Arthurian literature accessible to a broader public, White inspired a new generation of Arthurian enthusiasts. Meanwhile new work in archaeology and its interpretation by scholars like Leslie Alcock and Geoffrey Ashe offered a more detailed picture of Arthur's place in history. The impluse to rewrite Arthur's story, not set in the high Middle Ages or in an imaginary pseudomedieval setting like White's, but in his original fifth or sixth-century location has inspired a large number of later twentieth-century novels. These treatments range from straightforward historical novels of early medieval

Britain to anti-romantic struggles to strip the Arthurian legend of any remaining shreds of idealism. At the other extreme, the rise of fantasy and science fiction, especially after J. R. R. Tolkien, allowed novelists to embellish the Arthurian world with new species of magic, extrasensory perception, and occult ceremony. Surveying the many visions of Arthur produced in the past four decades, then, requires both discipline and adaptability on the part of critics and readers.

Arthurian literature of the 1950s. In the 1950s the Arthurian legend has also surfaced briefly in the works of a number of important writers whose main interests lay elsewhere. Vladimir Nabokov reused Chrétien de Troyes's Lancelot in a science-fiction short story, "Lance," in 1952, with Lancelot's crossing of the sword bridge now a space traveler's exploit. Among poets, Ezra Pound, who had already had a hand in editing T. S. Eliot's *Waste Land,* pillaged Layamon's *Brut* in *Section: Rock Drill—85–95—los cantares* (1955) to comment on vanishing British traditions and the changing role of the poet in the modern world. Two years later, Thom Gunn experimented with the Arthurian wizard in "Merlin in the Cave: He Speculates without a Book." Geoffrey Hill's short lyric "Merlin" in *For the Unfallen* (1959) names Arthur, Elaine, Modred, and Logres in two stanzas describing the magic by which the "outnumbering dead" are transformed into new life. Among the many brief Arthurian lyrics scattered through the poetry of the later twentieth century, this is one of the most successful.

The Natural (1952), Bernard Malamud's first novel, is intermittently classed by its perplexed critics among Arthurian works, and then discarded because no explicit Arthurian connections are stressed in the narrative. Nevertheless, that effective work deserves to be mentioned here as a powerful recasting of the grail quest in a twentieth-century American setting. Its ill-fated and innocent hero, the baseball player Roy Hobbs, continues the Perceval tradition in an original mode. Unlike the majority of its medieval predecessors and the Robert Redford film based on it, Malamud's grail quest ends in failure; in this respect it seems related more closely to Tennyson's "Holy Grail" and David Lodge's *Small World.* Their ultimate goal eludes each of these heroes as they make the wrong choice, never learning quite enough from their interminable wanderings.[28]

The main stream of Arthurian works published in the 1950s manifests the trend toward archaeological realism, replacing Arthur in the early Middle Ages. The image of that era naturally varies according to the author's attitude and sources. Henry Treece's novels for children and adults, *The Eagles Have Flown* (1954) and *The Great Captains* (1956) stress the brutality of sixth-century Britain. Arthur, for all his Roman antecedents, is as ferocious a warlord as any of his Saxon enemies. The effect is that of a strong reaction against the idealized high Middle Ages of nineteenth-century medievalism, charging instead into grinding realism, and, in some instances, out the other side into antiromantic fantasies.[29]

The English historical novelist Rosemary Sutcliffe gives a more balanced view of the sixth century in her Carnegie-medal-winning novel for children, *The Lantern Bearers* (1959).[30] Its hero, Aquila, deserts his troop of Roman auxiliaries to stay in Britain with his family, only to be captured in a Jutish raid and carried off to thralldom in his captors' European homeland. Through his embittered eyes, Sutcliffe surveys first the Saxons, then their ally Vortigern, as he is seduced by Hengist's daughter Rowena, and finally, after Aquila's escape, the Roman and Celtic forces of Prince Ambrosius. As Aquila mistrustfully rebuilds his life among Ambrosius's warriors, Sutcliffe also shows us the boyhood and youth of Arthur, here called Artos, Ambrosius's bastard nephew. The historical research is accurate and gracefully presented for the most part, interpreting Geoffrey of Monmouth in the light of modern archaeology. Aquila's psychological scars and their healing are also believably discussed. As a writer of English historical fiction for children, Rosemary Sutcliffe follows in the distinguished line of Rudyard Kipling's *Puck of Pook's Hill*. When she is not weighed down too heavily with description or pathos, she is a worthy successor, to be ranked among the best historical novelists at work in English.

On a lighter note, in 1955 Naomi Mitchison's *To the Chapel Perilous* brought a squad of reporters to cover the quest of the Holy Grail. The resulting satire mocks the foibles of the modern journalist more than the vagaries of the Arthurian legend.[31]

Arthur of the 1960s. The 1960s witnessed a rising interest in fantasy and science fiction, though older forms of Arthurian literature also continued to receive contributions. Rosemary Sutcliffe's historical novel *Sword at Sunset* (1963) picks up the narrative of *The Lantern Bearers* in a more ambitious adult narrative told from the point of view of Artos himself.[32] The constraints of accommodating existing tradition give *Sword at Sunset* less liberty of movement than *The Lantern Bearers*. Still, Sutcliffe portrays an Arthur who is a solid and in many ways endearing figure. Her novel should rank among the most successful attempts to retell the full Arthurian legend in the context of sixth-century Britain.

The opposite movement toward the modern-dress Arthurian narrative continued as well, notably in Sir Arthur Quiller-Couch's *Castle Dor,* completed posthumously by Daphne de Maurier (1961).[33] In the Cornish locale associated by tradition with the Tristan legend, Castle Dor, Quiller-Couch's novel shows the love triangle reenacted by modern characters. For Quiller-Couch, theirs is a tragedy of fate, intensified by its repetition. His critcs have marveled over the closeness with which Quiller-Couch follows the Tristan story and the number of traditional motifs he manages to include. Still, *Castle Dor* is more than a tour de force of modernization. It works as a tragic romance, harnessing the ancient story to powerful ends.

To the 1960s also belong Alan Garner's two forceful children's fantasies, *The Wierdstone of Brisingamen* (1960) and *The Moon of Gomrath* (1963).[34] Both are built upon the local legend that King Arthur and his knights are asleep in a cave near Alderley Edge in Cheshire, waiting to ride out and save England in a future crisis. The wizard who guards the sleepers in Garner's works recalls Merlin, though he is named Cadellin Silverbrow. He and the two children who discover his cave are confronted by the forces of evil in the person of the Morrigan, the ancient Irish goddess of battle once associated by some scholars with Morgan le Fay. Again, the Arthurian identification is not explicit or necessary here. Without adhering too strictly to traditional Arthurian plots or characters, Garner makes imaginative use of Celtic and Scandinavian mythologies. Students of Arthurian literature may be particularly interested in his interpretation of "The Spoils of Annwyn" in *The Moon of Gomrath.* His fantasies work as fast-paced suspense stories, but also as imaginative meditations on the impact of the supernatural on the human beings who are changed by their involvement with it.

A very different author of fantasy and science fiction, André Norton, found Arthurian details useful in two works published in the 1960s. In *Witch World* (1963) the Siege Perilous, now an ancient Celtic stone of power, provides the hero with an escape route from earth to another universe. In *Steel Magic* (1965) a group of children transported to Avalon carry out a series of character-testing quests for Arthurian magical objects, among them Excalibur.[35]

Arthurian literature of the 1970s. With the 1970s came the real explosion of interest in Arthur. The movement is transatlantic, finding enthusiastic participants in England and North America. The early 1970s continued the lines of development made apparent in the work of Garner and Norton during the 1960s. André Norton's *Merlin's Mirror* (1975) plays on the idea of Merlin, not as the devil's son, but as the son of an extraterrestrial being. His magic is rationalized as advanced technology, and the conclusion leaves him and Arthur awaiting the moment of their return, snug in their life-support system.[36]

At least some credit for the wave of popular Arthurian literature in the late 1970s and early 1980s should be given to Mary Stewart. The immense commerical success of her four Arthurian historical novels, published between 1970 and 1983, represents both a continuation and departure from her earlier Gothic romances. Her trilogy *The Crystal Cave* (1970), *The Hollow Hills* (1973), and *The Last Enchantment* (1979) is narrated by Merlin himself, here Ambrosius's illegitimate son.[37] It stands as the first in a series of Arthurian trilogies, modeled perhaps on White and Tolkien, and continuing in the works of Bradshaw, Canning, Godwin, Monaco, and Sharan Newman. Indeed, the trilogy should probably be identified as the dominant Arthurian genre of the 1970s and 1980s. In many ways, it carries its readers back to the three-volume novels of the eighteenth century.

Mary Stewart's Arthurian legends are set in the sixth century. Her interest in the religious plurality of the period looks forward to Marion Zimmer Bradley's *Mists of Avalon,* though in Stewart's novels Mithraism, Christianity, and the Druids coexist a good deal more peaceably than in that later work. Deliberate in their pace by comparison with most other Arthurian novels, Stewart's three Merlin narratives travel from Merlin's conception to Arthur's early reign, across the material of Malory's book 1. Like many later twentieth-century writers, Mary Stewart is interested in explaining the legends. While Merlin himself is endowed with extrasensory perception, "the Sight," his true stock in trade is science, not magic. Stewart returned to finish Arthur's story in *The Wicked Day* (1983).[38] That novel is centered around Mordred, no longer the epitome of evil, but a generally well-intentioned pragmatist, a victim of birth and destiny.

John Steinbeck's unfinished *Acts of King Arthur,* published posthumously in 1976, really belongs to the later 1950s, when Steinbeck was actively at work on it.[39] Steinbeck started out to rewrite the *Morte Darthur* in modern English, but by the time he attacked "Gawain, Ewain, and Marhalt," and "The Book of Sir Lancelot," he had shifted by imperceptible degrees into an original reworking of Malory's narrative. Steinbeck ends with his rather slow Lancelot's discovery of his feelings for Guinevere. Many of Steinbeck's inventions are attractive. He develops the characterization of the old, middle-aged, and young damsels who guide Gawain, Ywain, and Marhalt on their adventures: as in Tennyson's "Gareth," the aim is to focus on stages of human life. This section of Steinbeck's work also offers us a hilariously self-absorbed Gawain. In "Sir Lancelot," Steinbeck's Kay is an embattled administrator, "nibbled to death by numbers." His abbess objects to chivalry as an intrusion upon the Church's authority, and his four sorceresses subject Lancelot to a series of stiff sexual temptations, perhaps ultimately based on the Judgment of Paris. "Sir Lancelot" is in fact unified by the theme of Lancelot's sexual awakening, as a series of adventures selected from Malory reveal the nature of his own unexplored passions to him.

A series of Steinbeck's letters on the subject of Arthurian literature in general and this project in particular, published with the incomplete *Acts of Arthur,* illuminate Steinbeck's views of Arthur and his reading of Malory. They may be usefully set against White's correspondence on similar issues. Perhaps it is needless to mention that Steinbeck was not an uncritical admirer of *The Once and Future King.* He saw White's book as "wondrously wrought," but aimed at immediate popularity rather than towards the timeless, mythic appeal of the original legends. The letters do not explain why Steinbeck never completed his own Arthurian project. Brewer and Taylor note shrewdly that at his rate of expansion a treatment of Malory's "whole book" would have been prohibitively long. As they also observe, the confrontation of Lancelot and Guinevere does provide a good stopping point.[40] Steinbeck may also have been stalled by the problem of untangling Malory's "Book of Sir Tristran," which immediately follows "Sir Lancelot."

Two other well-regarded American novelists also published Arthurian works during the 1970s. Walker Percy's *Lancelot* (1978) is, like *The Natural,* a modern American grail novel.[41] Percy's narrative is centered on the Hollywood film industry. Its protagonist, a former Louisiana civil rights lawyer now confined to a mental institution, narrates the dispiriting tale of his quest for evil, focused on his wife's infidelities. Essentially, Percy reverses the direction of the grail quest to produce a negative image of the tradition. He uses legendary materials to add a mythic dimension to this hero's rage, disillusionment, and madness. The last item in particular finds emphatic precedent in Malory and his thirteenth-century French sources. In the same year, Thomas Berger published an Arthurian work almost completely opposite in character. His *Arthur Rex: A Legendary Novel* (1978) attempts to inflate Malory and an interesting variety of less commonly known medieval Arthurian sources into a comic epic in prose, with the assistance of violent blasts of burlesque.[42] Berger's use of archaic diction for comic effect is not uniformly successful with his readers, but critics have generally applauded this original vision of the Arthurian world. Berger's Gawaine certainly should rank among the most interesting in modern literature.

In children's literature the principal Arthurian work of the 1970s is Susan Cooper's series of five Arthurian fantasies, *Over Sea, Under Stone* (1965), *The Dark Is Rising* (1973; a 1974 Newbery Honor Book), *Greenwitch* (1974), *The Grey King* (1975; Newbery award winner), and *Silver on the Tree* (1977).[43] The degree of fantasy fluctuates from one of Cooper's volumes to the next as they shift between human and superhuman protagonists. In the first novel three children assist Merlin in recovering the grail, which is also sought by the powers of evil. Cooper's Merlin, disguised as a modern professor of archaeology, remains among the most convincing in recent Arthurian literature. The second novel introduces us to Will Stanton, a boy endowed with magical powers as the youngest of the Old Ones, a race of immortal beings standing in opposition to the Dark, the forces of destruction in Cooper's scheme. Merlin and other legendary figures are seen as belonging to one side or the other, so that the Arthurian legend itself becomes an episode in a continuing struggle between cosmic forces of good and evil. A majestic Arthur, Guinevere, and their lost son Bran figure in *The Grey King* and *Silver on the Tree*. Throughout the series the place of humanity in the cosmic order is a matter of debate. The relations between ordinary humans and beings with magical skills become sources of tension. In a way, Cooper picks up the problem where Alan Garner left off, and carries it to a difficult conclusion.

While these varied works may be the most successful Arthurian narratives of the 1970s in literary or commercial terms, this list by no means exhausts the astonishing production of Arthurian works in that decade, with 1978–79 as the crest of a tidal wave of interest in Arthur that has not yet altogether subsided. Victor Canning's 1978 *Crimson Chalice* united three earlier Arthurian novels: *The Crimson Chalice* (1976), *The Circle of the Gods* (1977), and *The Immortal Wound* (1978).[44] Canning treats the early Middle Ages and the Arthurian legend alike with a good deal of freedom, supplying Arthur with new parents for no easily apparent reason. Originality for its own sake might seem to be a factor in this decision. The American writer Richard Monaco's Parsival trilogy comprises *Parsival or a Knight's Tale* (1977), *The Grail*

War (1979), and *The Final Quest* (1980).[45] Monaco begins with Wolfram von Eschenbach and Wagner as his main sources in the first volume, but rapidly diverges from them to paint a brutal picture of life in the Waste Land. The grail knights' enemy Clinschor apparently represents Hitler. Interestingly, as in Tennyson, the quest of the Holy Grail leads its participants to neglect their domestic responsibilities, though otherwise the *Idylls of the King* and Monaco have few points of agreement. Finally, Robert Nye's erotic *Merlin* (1979) provides perhaps the ultimate illustration of the malleability of Arthurian legend, if such a demonstration were still necessary.[46]

A comic high point of the 1970s for many English and American audiences was provided by the film *Monty Python and the Holy Grail* (1975), directed by Terry Gilliam and Terry Jones, which sends up the conventions of chivalric romance in perhaps the most knowledgeable parody of its subject since Chaucer's *Sir Thopas*. A series of striking French films of the 1970s, Yvan Lagrange's *Tristan et Iseult* (1972), Robert Bresson's *Lancelot du Lac* (1974), and Eric Rohmer's *Perceval* (1978) reflect a soberer attitude toward the legends and their modern viewers.[47]

The 1980s: Arthur up to the present. The first half of the 1980s has been marked by a gradual decline in the production of Arthurian works, though the current of new ideas has not been exhausted by any means. The decade began impressively with Parke Godwin's *Firelord* (1980), like Sutcliffe's *Sword at Sunset* effectively narrated by Arthur.[48] Godwin's novel parallels Sutcliffe's again in its interest in meetings between the Arthurian characters and "fairies," a diminutive ancient race perplexing its British supplanters. In Godwin they are "the Prydn," beings of the Celtic other world. Here, Arthur's liaison with Morgana and begetting of Mordred take place in this other world. Godwin's Arthur reveals an active sense of humor, uncommon in representations of Arthur since *Culhwch and Olwen*. Overall, *Firelord* should be ranked among the strongest Arthurian narratives in this competitive and crowded period. Its sequel, *Beloved Exile* (1984), continues the story in an unusual direction by describing Guinevere's life after Arthur's death. The third novel in the series, *The Last Rainbow* (1985), really concerns Saint Patrick, and, peripherally, Ambrosius Aurelianus, acting as a preface to Arthur.

As the decade continued, Gillian Bradshaw's trilogy, *Hawk of May* (1980), *Kingdom of Summer* (1981), and *In Winter's Shadow* (1982), and Sharan Newman's trilogy, *Guinevere* (1981), *The Chessboard Queen*

(1984), and *Guinevere Evermore* (1985), shift their attention away from Arthur to other legendary figures.[49] Bradshaw attempts with reasonable success to rehabilitate Gawain as a hero, stressing his links with Celtic sun mythology to present Gwalchmai as a warrior in the service of light, in contrast with his mother Morgause's darkness. Newman offers a rare picture of the Roman Guinevere from her early adolescence, when she is initially portrayed as a dreamer distracted by a unicorn.

In film, John Boorman's *Excalibur* (1981) met with popular and critical applause for its ambitious chronicle of Arthurian history from Arthur's conception to his last battle.[50] The narrative is necessarily much compressed, consolidating Morgan le Fay, Morgause, and Vivien in a single villainess, Morgana. Making King Arthur into the wounded grail king and his kingdom into the Waste Land also keeps the narrative centered on a manageable number of characters. Malory is credited as the film's chief source, but *Excalibur* owes something to *Camelot* for its Galahad-like Lancelot, to the Tristan legends for the tryst in the forest that is transferred here to Lancelot and Guinevere, and to Tennyson for the idea of a last meeting between Arthur and Guinevere, though in Boorman's film Guinevere fortunately remains on her feet. Nicol Williamson's half-comic Merlin with his steel cap, furs, and staccato delivery, who returns for a final duel with Morgana, may also owe something to T. H. White. Architecturally, visually, and aurally, the film is powerful. It can be criticized as, perhaps, too eclectic a mixture of ingredients, as well as censured for its own tinge of gratuitous cruelty, reflected in the wholly unrealistic rape of Igerne by an Uther in full plate armor that is presented as the first major incident of the film.

Before the eighties neither the detective novel nor science fiction had distinguished itself for any major contribution to the Arthurian legend. C. J. Cherryh's *Port Eternity* (1982) remedied one of these gaps in memorable style.[51] Cherryh's Arthurian characters are genetically engineered "made people" modeled after principal figures in Tennyson's *Idylls of the King*. These beings and their self-indulgent mistress are drawn into reenacting the Arthurian legend in earnest when their spacecraft is trapped in limbo and they are confronted by threatening alien powers. Cherryh's use of Tennyson as a primary Arthurian source is refreshing, and it is pleasant to note how well Tennyson's Arthurian characters react to outer space. Innovating in a different direction, Roderick MacLeish's fantasy *Prince Ombra* (1982) uses the primary device of reincarnation to depict its young hero, Bentley Ellicott, as the twentieth-century embodiment of Arthur, David, and other heroes of the past, returned to confront the evil spirit Prince Ombra, once Modred and Goliath.[52] Phillis Ann Karr's Arthurian detective novel, *Idylls of the Queen* (1982), goes back to Malory for its main event, the poisoning of Sir Patrise at Guinevere's banquet.[53] Karr's work makes a major attempt to rehabilitate Sir Kay, who tells the story. Karr also sympathizes with Mordred and Morgan le Fay, perhaps more than with the conventional protagonists of Arthurian tradition. Similar tendencies are, of course, also at work in Mary Stewart's *Wicked Day* (1983).

While King Arthur had been a fixture in the American Sunday comic strips since Hal Foster's *Prince Valiant: In the Days of King Arthur* began its long run in 1951, in 1982 Mike W. Barr and Brian Bolland issued the first of a series of twelve comic books entitled *Camelot 3000,* in which the Arthurian characters return to battle Morgan le Fay and her army of insectlike alien invaders.[54] Naturally, the old conflicts develop between Lancelot, Guinevere, and Arthur, and between Arthur, Merlin, and Morgan, while Tristram must cope with the inconvenient fact that he has been reincarnated as a woman. *Camelot 3000* offers a striking combination of science fiction and Arthurian tradition, falling somewhere between popular literature, art, and dramatization.

The most widely read Arthurian novel of the early 1980s may well be Marion Zimmer Bradley's *Mists of Avalon* (1982).[55] Bradley follows a number of the women of Arthurian legend in her novel, but her main interest rests with Morgaine, again Arthur's half-sister. A major theme of this long fantasy novel is the conflict between advancing Christianity and the Celtic worship of the mother goddess, directed from the secret island of Avalon near Glastonbury by a matriarchal line of high priestesses who bear the title "Lady of the Lake." "Merlin," too, is not a personal name here but the title of the principal Druid. Since even today far too little is known for certain about the nature of Celtic paganism, Bradley uses Frazier's *Golden Bough,* a variety of archaeological and anthropological sources, and her own imagination to create an interesting feminist religion. The christianity of the Romanized Celts is presented as intolerant, paternalistic, and chilly, at least as Morgaine sees it. Bradley's work is unusual in giving Morgan le Fay and her sisters voices and rationalizations for their actions. Her insecure Guinevere is disappointing to us as well as to Morgaine, but others, Igraine, Vivien, and Morgause, for instance, are more prepossessing. While Marion Zimmer Bradley uses Malory's basic plot, its events are explained by means of her system, and Arthur's acceptance of Excalibur, the begetting of Mordred by Arthur on Morgaine rather than Morgause, and even the Holy Grail are invested, or perhaps reinvested, with pagan significance. Bradley's innovative use of female points of view has been especially instrumental in gaining her work its wide readership, though this rising interest in female characters can be traced in Sharan Newman and others as well, in a way recalling Tennyson and the Pre-Raphaelites' fascination with female Arthurian figures. The bulk and comprehensiveness of *The Mists of Avalon* demand a persistent reader; Bradley's imaginative liberties with historical evidence also require some forebearance on the part her audience.

For the even more dauntless reader of fantasy, a second Richard Monaco series, *Runes* (1984) and *Broken Stone* (1985), describes the adventures of Arthur's parents, followed by those of Arturus and Morga (Morgan), with further developments still to come.[56]

David Lodge's *Small World* (1984) returns the Arthurian legend to the twentieth century.[57] Lodge's sequel to his non-Arthurian 1975 novel, *Changing Places,* translates the quest of the Holy Grail into the pursuit of academic glory by a group of roving professors and students of literature on the run between international academic conferences. This is a Percival romance that deserves to be mentioned as one of the most inventive Arthurian comedies of the twentieth century. Traditional motifs are developed with verve. Lodge's hero, the young Irish poet Persse McGarigle, still must ask his crucial question, here at a New York meeting of the Modern Language Association. The Waste Land, the Fisher King, or at least Professor Arthur Kingfisher, and the dangerous Fulvia Morgana all make effective appearances. Here, again, Arthur himself becomes the sterile Fisher King of the grail quest, continuing one of the more popular Arthurian economies of our era. The novel works both as acute social satire and as grail romance, with an open-ended conclusion as Persse begins a new quest. If its academic focus gives its critics the distinct impression that they are biting their own tails, so much the better. This unexpected confection again demonstrates the vitality of the Arthurian legend as it approaches the end of its fourteenth century of existence.

Conclusion

From at least 500 A.D. to the present, the legend of Arthur has held its audience. Arthur has survived periods of disbelief or neglect, reappearing reliably, often at his own funeral. The secret of Arthur's enduring acclaim does not rest in any single facet of his legend, but in a quintessential combination of qualities. As the fantastic collaborative project that is Arthurian literature has developed over the centuries, the legend's potentialities have asserted themselves according to the changing preoccupations of successive eras. No approach has completely lost its validity. The process seems to be additive; nothing is ever lost beyond recall.

First, perhaps, Arthur himself deserves mention as the primary contributor to his own success. As a central character, King Arthur enjoys most of the advantages, and none of the limitations, of a well-established historical figure like Charlemagne. He appeals to his audience's national feeling, but not in a way that makes him the exclusive property of a single group. As the hope of the Britons, a dispersed people, Arthur has been granted a fame that transcends existing national boundaries. This paradox of defeat makes Arthur available to a wider audience than many other national heroes have found. At the same time, he does have powerful national and geographical associations that have always been appreciated in Arthurian literature. The balance of history and legend in the story of Arthur gives him patriotic status and international currency at the same time.

From a very early point in its existence, the Arthurian legend has betrayed strong utopian inclinations. Arthur is presented as the ideal military leader, later as the ideal ruler. His band of heroes gather in a court that becomes, as Camelot, the mirror of an ordered civilization. Camelot's fall is the fall of human aspiration toward a perfected society. This innate tendency of the narrative has enabled Arthurian literature to carry a large quantity of varied political or allegorical freight without undue discomfort. Certain writers have undoubtedly abused their opportunities in this direction; a disproportionate amount of questionable Arthurian literature has resulted from inept attempts to exploit Camelot's utopian possibilities. Nevertheless, the Arthurian legend's usefulness to political and social philosophies has generated and continues to generate a great deal of interest in King Arthur and his court.

Some of the appeal of the Arthurian legend is due to the romance structure. This factor may be the least recognized by modern critics dealing with later Arthurian works. Thanks to Geoffrey of Monmouth, Chrétien de Troyes, and Sir Thomas Malory, the episodic, thematically linked narrative pattern basic to many types of medieval romance is ingrained in Arthurian literature. This, more than anything else, may allow the legend to welcome new characters, adventures, and interpretations. More restrictive narrative forms can be far less accommodating. The story of Arthur keeps this faculty of friendliness to expansion and adaptation even when it is reshaped to fit later genres.

Another key to the success of Arthur's legend is its spiritual dimension. Arthur himself may always have been a messianic hero in some sense. The legend of his potential return allows him to be a savior of the future as well as the past. For Caxton, the mystical drama of the Holy Grail placed Arthur and his knights first in the pantheon of Christian chivalric heroes, ahead of their medieval rivals, Charlemagne and the leaders of the First Crusade. The nineteenth and twentieth centuries rediscovered the appeal of these supernatural adventures after three centuries of Protestant aversion. Arthur's knights function as explorers traversing an apocalyptic landscape.

The psychological drama of King Arthur's court unquestionably captured the interest of a large audience since twelfth-century authors began to emphasize this dimension of Arthurian romance. The story of King Arthur is about human relations. Its characters are at once larger than life and emphatically believable at the same time. Although there have been notable exceptions, traditionally few Arthurian characters are flawlessly admirable or completely despicable. The most successful share our temptations and crises. The answers are never easy. A sophisticated awareness of the complexities of human interconnections seems to be built into the simplest Arthurian narratives. Universal and insoluble tensions of passion, temptation, and restraint control the basic plot.

Later readers coming to any medieval work share the nineteenth century's appreciation of its strangeness, wonder, and remoteness, which is, for us, part of the fantasy. Since the days of *Culhwch and Olwen,* Arthurian literature has always offered its share of magic, however often it may be deemphasized, rationalized, or explained away. Merlin threatens Arthur's position as the central figure of the legend as much today as when he first charmed Geoffrey of Monmouth, perhaps more.

Unquestionably, the story of Arthur ranks as a great tragedy. At the same time, it is an unusual kind of tragedy, preserving hope for the future, or perhaps for eternity, in the teeth of disaster. Perhaps here most of all, the legend of Arthur betrays its origins in the Christian Middle Ages, an era some scholars describe as theologically incapable of complete despair. Because Arthur does not vanish into irretrievable ruin, because Gawain, Guinevere, and Lancelot are given the opportunity for redemption, the legend retains a kind of long-term optimism that attracts the most sceptical reader in spite of his or her pragmatic instincts.

Twentieth-century scholars recognize Arthur's story, historical or not, as one of the primary myths of Western civilization. Twentieth-century authors have stressed, for the most part, the key dualities inherent in Arthur's traditional narrative. King Arthur's battles represent, for our time, the struggle of civilization against barbarism, good against evil, reason against emotion, the spiritual against the earthly, family against society, friendship against love, Christian against pagan. Perhaps this tendency says as much about our own litigious and combative age as it does about the Arthurian legend.

For too many reasons, the history of the Round Table has never lost its attraction. Is it really the Arthurian legend itself that maintains its hold on the imagination, or should credit go to its literature? The tale's ability to compel attention has unquestionably been enhanced by the many inspired tellers who have adorned it over the centuries. King Arthur's standing today results from their successive efforts, as much as from his story's own attractions. In fact, the myth and the myth-ographers cannot be separated. Readers still care about the fate of Camelot because of Geoffrey of Monmouth, Malory, and Tennyson, but also because of Arthur, Lancelot, and Guinevere. The Arthurian legend enters its fifteenth century with undiminished power and authority, a remarkable achievement for a monarch, or a myth, of any age.

Notes and References

Chapter One

1. Sheppard S. Frere, *Britannia: A History of Roman Britain,* rev. ed. (London: Routledge & Kegan Paul, 1978), 14–15, 248–72. Peter Salway, *Roman Britain* (Oxford: Oxford University Press, 1981), chap. 16, 446–501. Anthony R. Birley, *The People of Roman Britain* (Berkeley and Los Angeles: University of California Press, 1980); C. J. Arnold, *Roman Britain to Saxon England* (Bloomington: Indiana University Press, 1984); John Morris, *The Age of Arthur* (New York: Scribner, 1973).

2. See Frere, *Britannia,* and Salway, *Roman Britain.*

3. On Roman religion and religious sites in Britain, see Frere, *Britannia,* 361–75; Arnold, *Roman Britain,* 142–56; Salway, *Roman Britain,* 665–739. See also John Darrah, *The Real Camelot: Paganism and the Arthurian Romances* (London: Thames & Hudson, 1981).

4. For Pelagius, see Birley, *People,* 154–56; Jaroslav Pelikan, *The Christian Tradition: A History of the Development of Doctrine,* vol. 1, *The Emergence of the Catholic Tradition (100–600)* (Chicago: University of Chicago Press, 1971), 313–31.

5. On relations between Britons and Gauls, see Salway, *Roman Britain,* and Geoffrey Ashe, " 'A Certain Very Ancient Book': Traces of an Arthurian Source of Geoffrey of Monmouth's *History," Speculum* 56 (1981):301–23.

6. Frere, *Britannia,* 409–10; Salway, *Roman Britain,* 442–43.

7. See J. N. L. Myres, *The English Settlements.* (Oxford: Clarendon Press, 1986).

8. David M. Wilson, ed., *The Archaeology of Anglo-Saxon England* (1976; reprint ed., Cambridge: Cambridge University Press, 1981).

9. David Dumville, "Sub-Roman Britain: History and Legend," *History* 62 (1977):173–92.

10. Gildas, *De excidio Brittanniae,* ed. and trans. Michael Winterbottom, in *History from the Sources,* vol. 7, *The Ruin of Britain* (Chichester, England: Phillimore, 1978).

11. On Roman federate troops, see Frere, *Britannia,* Birley, *People,* Ashe, "Certain Book."

12. Gildas, *De excidio,* 98; *Ruin of Britain,* 27–28.

13. C. Scott Littleton and Ann C. Thomas, "The Sarmatian Connection," *Journal of American Folklore* (1978) offer a hypothesis connecting Arthur with an earlier Roman commander in Britain, Artorius Castus.

14. Gildas, *De excidio,* 98; *Ruin of Britain,* 28.

15. Leslie Alcock, *Arthur's Britain* (London: Penguin, 1971); Richard Barber, *The Figure of King Arthur* (London: Longman, 1972).

16. On Gildas's dating, see Ashe, "Certain Book," and Michael Lapidge and David Dumville, eds., *Gildas: New Approaches* (Woodbridge, Suffolk, England: Boydell & Brewer, 1984).

17. Bede, *Opera historica,* ed. Charles Plummer (London: Clarendon Press, 1896); Bede, *A History of the English Church and People,* trans. Leo Shirley-Price, rev. ed. (1968; reprint ed., London: Penguin, 1968).

18. Nennius, *Historia Brittonum,* ed. and trans. John Morris, in *History from the Sources,* vol. 8, *British History and the Welsh Annals* (Chichester, England: Phillimore, 1980). See also David Dumville, "The Historical Value of the *Historia Brittonum.*" *Arthurian Literature* 6 (1986):1–26.

19. Frere, *Britannia,* 427.

20. For a contrary view, see Rachel Bromwich's articles in *Studia Celtica* (1875–76) and Barber, *Figure of Arthur.*

21. Nennius, *Historia,* 76; *British History,* 35.

22. Ibid., 83; 42.

23. *Annales Cambriae,* in ibid., 85; 45.

24. Ashe, "Certain Book," 305.

25. Richard L. Brengle, trans., *Arthur King of Britain: History, Chronicle, Romance, and Criticism* (Englewood Cliffs, N.J.: Prentice-Hall, 1964), 8. William of Malmesbury, *Gesta regum Anglorum,* in *Willelmi Malmesbiriensis monachi de gestis regum Anglorum libri quinque,* ed. William Stubbs, 2 vols. (London: Eyre & Spottiswoode, 1887–89).

26. Gerald of Wales, *Giraldi Cambrensis opera,* ed. J. S. Brewer, J. F. Dimock, and G. F. Warner, Rolls Series, 8 vols. (London: Longman, 1861–92); Gerald of Wales, *The Journey through Wales and the Description of Wales,* trans. Lewis Thorpe (London: Penguin, 1978).

27. Translated by James J. Wilhelm in *The Romance of Arthur,* ed. James J. Wilhelm and Laila Gross (New York: Garland, 1984), 10.

28. See Alcock, *Arthur's Britain.*

29. See ibid. on Glastonbury excavations.

30. Kenneth Jackson, *The Gododdin: The Oldest Scottish Poem* (Edinburgh: Edinburgh University Press, 1969).

31. See the work of Morton W. Bloomfield and Charles Dunn on the poet in early societies. Gwyn Williams, *An Introduction to Welsh Poetry* (London: Faber & Faber, 1953).

32. *The Gododdin,* trans. John K. Bolland, *Romance of Arthur,* ed. Wilhelm and Gross, 14.

33. Ibid., 14–15; Nennius, *Historia,* 76; *British History,* 35.

34. Thomas Jones, "The Black Book of Carmarthen 'Stanzas of the Graves,' " *Proceedings of the British Academy* 53 (1967): 97–137. A. O. H.

Jarman, "The Arthurian Allusions in the Black Book of Carmarthen," in *The Legend of Arthur in the Middle Ages: Studies Presented to A. H. Diverres,* ed. P. B. Grout, R. A. Lodge, C. E. Pickford, and E. K. C. Varty (London: Boydell & Brewer, 1983), 99–112; *The Poems of Taliesin,* ed. J. E. Caerwyn Williams and Ifor Williams (Dublin: Dublin Institute for Advanced Studies, 1968).

35. Williams, *Introduction,* 5.

36. For Geraint, see the *Black Book of Carmarthen,* ed. Brynly F. Roberts, in *Astudiaethau ar yr Hengerdd: Studies in Early Welsh Poetry.* (Cardiff: University of Wales, 1978).

37. "The Stanzas of the Graves," trans. Bolland, in *Romance of Arthur,* ed. Wilhelm and Gross, 17.

38. Ibid., 18.

39. Ibid., 20.

40. Roger Sherman Loomis, *Wales and the Arthurian Legend* (Cardiff: University of Wales Press, 1956).

41. "The Spoils of Annwn," trans. Bolland, *Romance of Arthur,* ed. Wilhelm and Gross, 22.

42. Rachel Bromwich, *Trioedd Ynys Prydein: The Welsh Triads,* rev. ed. (Cardiff: University of Wales Press, 1978); Bromwich, "The Welsh Triads," in *Arthurian Literature in the Middle Ages,* ed. Roger Sherman Loomis (Oxford: Clarendon Press, 1959), 44–51.

43. Bromwich, *Trioedd* no. 80. Wilhelm, 25.

44. J. Gwenogvryn Evans, ed., *The White Book Mabinogion* (Pwllheli: n.p. 1907); Sir John Rhys and J. Gwenogvryn Evans, *The Text of the Mabinogion and Other Welsh Tales from the Red Book of Hergest* (Oxford: J. G. Evans, 1890); Patrick K. Ford, trans., *The Mabinogi and Other Medieval Welsh Tales* (Berkeley and Los Angeles: University of California Press, 1977), introduction. English translations of the *Mabinogion* include those of Patrick K. Ford, Lady Guest (1849), Jeffrey Gantz (1976), and Gwyn and Thomas Jones (1949).

45. See Ford, Introduction, and his article in *The Arthurian Encyclopedia,* ed. Norris J. Lacy et al. (New York: Garland, 1986), 124–27.

46. See Ford, Introduction, and Richard M. Loomis, in *Romance of Arthur,* ed. Wilhelm and Gross, 28.

47. See Kenneth Hurlstone Jackson, "Arthur in Early Welsh Verse," in *Arthurian Literature,* ed. Loomis, 12–19.

48. Gerald of Wales, *Itinerarium Cambriae,* in *Giraldi Cambrensis opera,* vi.

49. Ashe, "Certain Book."

50. E. K. Chambers, *Arthur of Britain* (London: Sidgwick & Jackson, 1927).

51. Geoffrey of Monmouth, *History of the Kings of Britain,* trans. Lewis Thorpe (London: Penguin, 1966); Geoffrey of Monmouth, *Vita Merlini,* ed. and trans. J. J. Parry (Urbana: University of Illinois Press, 1925).

52. On Geoffrey of Monmouth's sources, see Ashe, "Certain Book," Stuart Piggott, "The Sources of Geoffrey of Monmouth," *Antiquity* 15 (1941); Chambers, *Arthur.*

53. See Chambers, *Arthur.*

54. Ashe, "Certain Book."

55. See Chambers, *Arthur.*

56. Ibid.

57. Mildred Leake Day, ed. and trans., *The Rise of Gawain, Nephew of Arthur (De ortu Waluuanii nepotis Arturi)* (New York: Garland, 1984). Henry of Huntingdon, *Epistola ad Warinum,* in *Chronicles of the Reigns of Stephen, Henry II, and Richard I,* ed. Richard Howlett (London: Longman, Trübner, 1885); Chambers, *Arthur.*

58. Wace, *Le Roman de Brut,* ed. I. Arnold, 2 vols. (Paris: SATF, 1938–40); Wace, *Le Roman de Rou,* ed. A. J. Holden, 3 vols. (Paris: SATF, 1970–73). Wace and Layamon, *Arthurian Chronicles,* trans. Eugene Mason (London: Dent, 1912).

59. On the manuscripts of Wace, see the editions listed above.

60. Layamon, *Brut,* ed. G. L. Brook and R. F. Leslie (London: Oxford University Press, 1963, 1978).

61. On Layamon's alliteration, see ibid.

62. William W. Kibler, "Wace," in *Arthurian Encyclopedia,* 615–16.

Chapter Two

1. Arthur R. Heiserman, *The Novel before the Novel: Essays and Discussions about the Beginnings of Prose Fiction in the West* (1977; reprint ed., Chicago: University of Chicago Press, 1980); Northrop Frye, *The Secular Scripture: A Study of the Structure of Romance* (Cambridge, Mass.: Harvard University Press, 1976); Roger Sherman Loomis, *The Development of Arthurian Romance* (New York: Harper & Row, 1963); Claude Luttrell, *The Creation of the First Arthurian Romances* (Evanston: Northwestern University Press, 1974); John Stevens, *Medieval Romance: Themes and Approaches* (London: Hutchinson, 1973); Eugène Vinaver, *The Rise of Romance* (Oxford: Oxford University Press, 1971).

2. Derek Brewer, *Symbolic Stories: Traditional Narratives of the Family Drama in English Literature.* (Cambridge: D. S. Brewer; Totowa, N.J.: Rowman & Littlefield, 1980); Georges Duby, *The Chivalrous Society,* trans., Cynthia Postan (1977; reprint ed., Berkeley and Los Angeles: University of California Press, 1980), 112–22.

3. On the audiences of the romance, see also Velma Richmond, *The Popularity of Middle English Romance* (Bowling Green, Ohio: Bowling Green

University Popular Press, 1975); Lee C. Ramsey, *Chivalric Romances: Popular Literature in Medieval England* (Bloomington: Indiana University Press, 1983).

4. Chrétien de Troyes, *Les Romans de Chrétien de Troyes,* Les Classiques français du moyen age, vol. 1, *Erec et Enide,* ed. Mario Roques (Paris: Champion, 1970); vol. 2, *Cligès,* ed. Alexandre Micha (Paris: Champion, 1958); vol. 3, *Le Chevalier de la charrete,* ed. Mario Roques (Paris: Champion, 1969); vol. 4, *Le Chevalier au lion,* ed. Mario Roques (Paris: Champion, 1970); *Le Roman de Perceval (Le Conte du Graal),* ed. William Roach (Paris and Geneva: Minard & Droz, 1959). For additional reading, see Douglas Kelly, *Chrétien de Troyes: An Analytic Bibliography* (London: Grant & Cutler, 1976); Jean Frappier, *Chrétien de Troyes* (Paris: Hatier, 1957); Norris J. Lacy, *The Craft of Chrétien de Troyes* (Leiden, Netherlands: Brill, 1980); L. T. Topsfield, *Chrétien de Troyes: A Study of the Arthurian Romances* (Cambridge: Cambridge University Press, 1981).

5. On Chrétien's treatment of Arthur, see Frappier, *Chrétien de Troyes,* Topsfield, *Chrétien de Troyes.*

6. Some recent translators include William W. Kibler, Ruth Harwood Cline, and Nigel Bryant. Important adaptations of Chrétien's works into other languages during the Middle Ages include the Middle High German romances of Hartmann von Aue, discussed in Peter Wapnewski, *Hartmann von Aue* 7th ed. (Stuttgart: Metzler, 1979). The relationship between Chrétien and the three Welsh romances, *Peredur, Owain,* and *Geraint* is more difficult to establish. See A. O. H. Jarman and Gwilym Rees Hughes, *A Guide to Welsh Literature* (Swansea, Wales: Davies, 1976), vol. 1.

7. See Jean Frappier, "Chrétien de Troyes," *Arthurian Literature,* ed. Loomis, 159.

8. See Norris J. Lacy, in *Arthurian Encyclopedia,* 106–7.

9. On the debate over courtly love, see Jean Frappier, *Amour courtois et table ronde* (Geneva: Droz, 1973); Moshé Lazar, *Armour courtois et "fin amors" dans la litterature du xiie siècle* (Paris: Klincksieck, 1964); F. X. Newman, ed., *The Meaning of Courtly Love* (Albany: State University of New York Press, 1968); and for a powerful but now disputed argument, C. S. Lewis, *The Allegory of Love* (1936; reprint ed., Oxford: Oxford University Press, 1976). The source causing most of the controversy is Andreas Capellanus, *The Art of Courtly Love,* trans. John Jay Parry (1941; reprint ed., New York: Norton, 1969).

10. Roger S. Loomis, *The Grail: From Celtic Myth to Christian Symbol* (Cardiff: University of Wales Press, 1963); Urban T. Holmes, *Chrétien, Troyes, and the Grail* (1959); Jessie L. Weston, *From Ritual to Romance* (Cambridge University Press, 1920); Jean Marx, *La Légende arthurienne et le graal* (Paris: Presses universitaires, 1952); D. D. R. Owen, *The Evolution of the Grail Legend* (Edinburgh and London: Glover & Boyd, 1968).

11. On the social circumstances of reading, see Janet Coleman, *Medieval Readers and Writers, 1350–1400* (New York: Columbia University Press, 1981).

12. See Loomis, ed. *Arthurian Literature;* William Roach, ed., *The Didot-Perceval* (Philadelphia: University of Pennsylvania Press, 1941); Richard O'Gorman, "The Prose Version of Robert de Boron's *Joseph d'Arimathie,"* *Romance Philology* 23 (1970):449–61; and O'Gorman's article in *Arthurian Encyclopedia,* 456–58.

13. H. Oskar Sommer, ed., *The Vulgate Version of the Arthurian Romances,* 8 vols. (Washington, D.C.: Carnegie Institution, 1908–16); E. Jane Burns, *Arthurian Fictions: Re-reading the Vulgate Cycle* (Columbus: Ohio State University Press, 1985); Loomis, ed., *Arthurian Literature,* 316–17.

14. See Elspeth Kennedy, ed., *Lancelot do Lac: The Non-cyclic Old French Prose Romance,* 2 vols. (Oxford: Clarendon Press, 1980); Alexandre Micha, ed., *Lancelot: roman en prose du xiie siècle,* 7 vols. (Geneva: Droz, 1978–80).

15. See Loomis, ed., *Arthurian Literature.*

16. See Albert Pauphilet, ed., *La Queste del Saint Graal* (Paris: Champion, 1923); Etienne Gilson's discussion of the theological background of the *Queste,* "La mystique de la grâce dans La queste del Saint Graal," reprinted in *Les Idées et les lettres* (Paris: J. Vrin, 1932), 56–91; P. M. Matarasso, trans., *The Quest of the Holy Grail* (1969; reprint ed., Harmondsworth, England: Penguin, 1976), introduction.

17. Loomis, ed., *Arthurian Literature;* Eugène Vinaver, ed., *The Works of Sir Thomas Malory,* 3 vols., rev. ed. (Oxford: Oxford University Press, 1967); 3:1657–58.

18. Loomis, ed., *Arthurian Literature.*

19. Alexandre Micha, ed., *Merlin, roman du xiiie siècle* (Geneva: Droz, 1979).

20. Fanni Bogdanow, *The Romance of the Grail: A Study of the Structure and Genesis of a Thirteenth-Century Arthurian Prose Romance* (Manchester: Manchester University Press, 1966); Fanni Bogdanow, "The *Suite du Merlin* and the Post-Vulgate *Roman du Graal,"* in *Arthurian Literature,* ed. Loomis, 325–35.

21. Keith Busby, *Gauvain in Old French Literature* (Amsterdam: Rodopi, 1980).

22. See Geoffrey Ashe, in *Arthurian Encyclopedia,* 566–67; Gertrude Schoepperle (Loomis), *Tristan and Isolt: A Study of the Sources of the Romance,* 2d ed., ed. R. S. Loomis (New York: Franklin, 1959); Sigmund Eisner, *The Tristan Legend: A Study in Sources* (Evanston: Northwestern University Press, 1969).

23. Marie de France, *Lais,* ed. Alfred Ewert (Oxford: Blackwell, 1960); Emanuel J. Michel, Jr., *Marie de France* (New York: Twayne, 1954).

24. Helaine Newstead, "The Origin and Growth of the Tristan Legend," in *Arthurian Literature,* ed. Loomis, 122–33; Béroul, *Le Roman de Tristan,* ed. Ernest Muret (Paris: Champion, 1962); Eilhart von Oberge, *Tristrant,* ed, Danielle Buschinger (Göppingen, Germany: Kummerle, 1976); Eilhart von Oberge, *Tristrant,* trans. J. W. Thomas (Lincoln: University of Nebraska Press, 1978); Thomas, *Les Fragments du roman de Tristan, poème du xiie siècle,* ed. B. H. Wind (Geneva: Droz, 1960); *The Saga of Tristram and Isönd,* trans. Paul Schach (Lincoln: University of Nebraska Press, 1973); Gottfried von Strassburg, *Tristan,* ed. Reinhold Bechstein, reedited by Peter Ganz (Wiesbaden: Brockhaus, 1978); Gottfried von Strassburg, *Tristan, with the Surviving Fragments of the Tristan of Thomas,* trans. A. T. Hatto (Harmondsworth, England: Penguin, 1974); Edmund G. Gardner, *The Arthurian Legend in Italian Literature* (London: Dent, 1930).

25. Michael Batts, *Gottfried von Strassburg* (New York: Twayne, 1971); W. T. H. Jackson, *The Anatomy of Love: The Tristan of Gottfried von Strassburg* (New York: Columbia University Press, 1971); C. Stephen Jaeger, *Medieval Humanism in Gottfried von Strassburg's "Tristan und Isolde"* (Heidelberg: Winter, 1977), and his article in the *Arthurian Encyclopedia,* 249–56.

26. Emmanuèle Baumgartner, *Le Tristan en prose: essai d'interpretation* (Geneva: Droz, 1975).

27. William A. Nitze and T. A. Jenkins, eds., *Le Haut Livre du Graal: Perlesvaus,* 2 vols. (Chicago: University of Chicago Press, 1932–37); Loomis, ed. *Arthurian Literature.*

28. See Loomis, ed., *Arthurian Literature;* Wolfram von Eschenbach, *Works,* ed. Karl Lachmann 6th ed., (Berlin: de Gruyter, 1926; reprint ed., 1965); Wolfram von Eschenbach, *Parzival,* ed. Albert Leitzmann, 6th ed., ed. Wilhelm Deinert, 5 vols. (Tübingen, Germany: Niemeyer, 1965); Wolfram von Eschenbach, *Parzival,* trans. A. T. Hatto (Harmondsworth, England: Penguin, 1980); James F. Poag, *Wolfram von Eschenbach* (New York: Twayne, 1972); Hugh Sackler, *An Introduction to Wolfram's "Parzifal"* (Cambridge: Cambridge University Press, 1963).

29. For *minne,* see A. Luderitz, *Die liebestheorie der Provençalen bei den minnesingern der stauferzeit* (1904); M. F. Ritchey, *Essays on the Mediaeval German Love Lyric* (1943).

30. See Loomis, ed., *Arthurian Literature;* and Busby, *Gauvain;* see also Wendelin Foerster, ed., *Le Chevaliers as deus espées* (Halle, Germany: Niemeyer, 1977); Heinrich von dem Türlin, *Diu Crône,* ed. G. H. F. Scholl (Stuttgart: 1852); Margaret Winters, ed., *Hunbaut* (Leiden, Netherlands: Brill, 1984); Mathias Friedwagner, ed., *La Vengeance Radiguel* (Halle, Germany: Niemeyer, 1909); R. C. Johnson and D. D. R. Owen, eds., *Two Old French Gawain Romances* (New York: Barnes & Noble, 1973); Brain Woledge, ed., *L'Atre perilleux* (Paris: Champion, 1936).

31. See W. J. Entwistle, *Arthurian Literature in the Literature of the Spanish Peninsula* (London: Dent, 1925); E. G. Gardner, *The Arthurian Legend in Italian Literature* (London: Dent; New York: E. P. Dutton, 1930); Marianne E. Kalinke, *King Arthur, North-by-Northwest: The Matière de Bretagne' in Old-Norse-Icelandic Romances* (Copenhagen: Reitzel, 1981); as well as Loomis, ed., *Arthurian Literature* and the *Arthurian Encyclopedia*.

32. Jean Froissart, *Méliador*, ed. A. Longnon, 3 vols. (Paris: Didot, 1895–99); Peter F. Dembowski, *Jean Froissart and his "Méliador": Context, Craft, and Sense* (Lexington, Ky.: French Forum, 1983).

33. H. L. D. Ward, *Catalogue of Romances in the Department of Manuscripts in the British Museum*, 3 vols. (London: British Museum, 1983); see also Ramsey, *Chivalric Romances*, and Coleman, *Books and Readers*.

34. See R. W. Ackerman, "English Rimed and Prose Romances," in *Arthurian Literature*, ed. Loomis; F. J. Child, ed., *The English and Scottish Popular Ballads* (Boston: Houghton Mifflin, 1884); *Merlin*, pts. 1–3, ed. Ernst A. Kock, 3 vols. (London: Oxford University Press, 1904, 1913, 1930). John W. Hales and F. J. Furnivall, eds., *Bishop Percy's Folio Manuscript: Ballads of Romances*, 3 vols. (London: Trübner, 1867–69), 1:103.

35. On the Auchinleck manuscript, see Laura Hibbard Loomis, "Chaucer and the Breton Lays of the Auchinleck Manuscript," *Studies in Philology* 38(1941):14–33.

36. Eugen Kölbing, ed. *Arthour and Merlin* (Heilbronn, Germany: Henninger, 1890); Ackerman, "English Rimed," 485–86; Henry Lovelich, *The History of the Holy Grail* (pts. 1–4), ed. F. J. Furnivall, 4 vols. (London: Trübner, 1874, 1875, 1877, 1878).

37. Albert B. Friedman and Norman T. Harrington, eds., *Ywain and Gawain* (London: Oxford University Press, 1964).

38. Thomas Chestre, *Libeaus desconus*, ed. Maldwyn Mills (London: Oxford University Press, 1969); Frederick Madden, ed., *Syre Gawayne* (London: Bannatyne Club, 1839); Auvo Kurvinen, ed., *Sir Gawain and the Carl of Carlisle in Two Versions*, Annales Academiae Scientiarum Fennicae, Series B 71.2 (Helsinki: 1951); Robert J. Gates, ed., *The Awntyrs off Arthure at the Tarne Wathelyne* (Philadelphia: University of Pennsylvania Press, 1969); Ralph Hanna III, ed., *The Awntyrs off Arthure at the Tarne Wathelyn* (Manchester: Manchester University Press, 1974); Roger Dahood, ed., *The Avowing of King Arthur* (New York: Garland, 1984).

39. D. B. Sands, ed., *Middle English Romances* (New York: Holt, Rinehart & Winston, 1966); L. Sumner, ed., *The Wedding of Sir Gawen and Dame Ragnell* (Northampton, Mass.: Smith College, 1924); see also John Jacobs Niles, *The Ballad Book* (Boston: Houghton Mifflin, 1961), 106–8 for a version of the ballad from North Carolina.

40. Geoffrey Chaucer, *Works,* ed. F. N. Robinson, 2d ed., (Boston: Houghton Mifflin, 1957); *The Wife of Bath's Prologue and Tale,* ed. J. Winny (Cambridge: Cambridge University Press, 1965); Derek Pearsall, *The Canterbury Tales* (London: Allen & Unwin, 1985), 86–91.

41. Larry D. Benson, ed., *King Arthur's Death* (Indianapolis: Bobbs-Merrill, 1974); P. F. Hissinger, ed., *Le Morte Arthure: A Critical Edition* (The Hague: Mouton, 1975); Richard A. Wertime, "The Theme and Structure of the Stanzaic *Morte Arthur,*" *PMLA* 87(1972):1075–82; Sharon E. Knopp, "Artistic Design in the stanzaic *Morte Arthur,*" *Journal of English Literary History* 45(1978):563–82.

42. See Benson, *King Arthur's Death;* Valerie Krishna, ed., *The Alliterative "Morte Arthure": A Critical Edition* (New York: Franklin, 1976); William Matthews, *The Tragedy of Arthur: A Study of the Alliterative "Morte Arthure"* (Berkeley and Los Angeles: University of California Press, 1960); Karl Heinz Göller, ed., *The Alliterative "Morte Arthure": A Reassessment of the Poem* (Woodbridge, Suffolk, England: Boydell & Brewer, 1981).

43. For basic reading on the Alliterative Revival, see David Lawton, ed., *Middle English Alliterative Poetry and Its Literary Background: Seven Essays* (Cambridge: D. S. Brewer; Totowa, N.J.: Boydell & Brewer, 1982), especially the essay by Derek Pearsall; J. P. Oakden, *Alliterative Poetry in Middle English,* 2 vols. (Manchester: Manchester University Press, 1930–35); Larry D. Benson, *Art and Tradition in "Sir Gawain and the Green Knight"* (New Brunswick, N.J.: Rutgers University Press, 1965).

44. See Larry D. Benson, *Malory's "Morte Darthur"* (Cambridge, Mass.: Harvard University Press, 1976), 189–90. Otto Cartellieri, *The Court of Burgundy,* trans. Malcolm Letts (1925; reprint ed., New York: Haskell House, 1970), 135–53.

45. David A. Lawton, "The Unity of Middle English Alliterative Poetry," *Speculum* 58 (1983):72–94.

46. J. R. R. Tolkien and E. V. Gordon, eds., *Sir Gawain and the Green Knight,* 2d ed., ed. Norman Davis (Oxford: Clarendon Press, 1967); Malcolm Andrew, *The Gawain-Poet: An Annotated Bibliography* (New York: Garland, 1979).

47. Donald R. Howard, "Structure and Symmetry in *Sir Gawain,*" in *Critical Studies of "Sir Gawain and the Green Knight,*" ed. Donald R. Howard and Christian K. Zacher (1968; reprint ed., Notre Dame, Ind.: University of Notre Dame Press, 1970), 159–173.

48. For different readings, see Howard and Zacher, *Critical Studies;* Benson, *Art and Tradition;* J. A. Burrow, *A Reading of "Sir Gawain and the Green Knight"* (London: Routledge & Kegan Paul, 1965).

49. Benson, *Art and Tradition;* Howard and Zacher, *Critical Studies;* Elizabeth Brewer, trans., *From Cuchulainn to Gawain: Sources and Analogues of "Sir Gawain and the Green Knight"* (Cambridge: Brewer, 1973).

Chapter Three

1. William Matthews, *The Ill-Framed Knight* (Berkeley and Los Angeles: University of California Press, 1966). For further information on this and other topics relating to Malory, see Page West Life, *Sir Thomas Malory and the "Morte Darthur"* (Charlottesville: University Press of Virginia, 1980).

2. Edward Hicks, *Sir Thomas Malory: His Turbulent Career* (1928; reprint ed., New York: Octagon Books, 1970). For a defense of Sir Thomas Malory of Newbold Revel that questions many of the more colorful accusations, see P. J. C. Field, "Thomas Malory: The Hutton Documents," *Medium Aevum* 48 (1979):213–39; "The Last Years of Sir Thomas Malory," *Bulletin of the John Rylands Library* 64 (1982):433–56.

3. Edmund Reiss, *Sir Thomas Malory* (Boston: Twayne, 1966), 17.

4. For example, see ibid., 17–20. Compare Johan Huizinga, *The Waning of the Middle Ages* (New York: Doubleday, 1953). For a more recent view of fifteenth-century life and literature with special reference to chivalry, see Maurice Keen, *Chivalry* (New Haven: Yale University Press, 1984).

5. Matthews, *Ill-Framed Knight,* 115–54.

6. Richard Griffith, "The Authorship Question Reconsidered: A Case for Thomas Malory of Papworth St. Agnes, Cambridgeshire," in *Aspects of Malory,* ed. T. Takamiya and D. S. Brewer (Cambridge: D. S. Brewer, 1981), 159–77.

7. Sir Thomas Malory, *Works,* ed. Eugène Vinaver (1971; reprint ed., Oxford: Oxford University Press, 1978), 110, 226, 726. This one-volume edition presents Vinaver's final revisions of his second three-volume edition of Malory. At his last word on textual matters, it is used for all quotations from Malory's text in this chapter (hereafter referred to as "Vinaver").

8. For Matthews's linguistic analysis, see *The Ill-Framed Knight,* 75–89, and Appendix D. For Chaucer's view of the southern reception of alliterative poetry, see the prologue to his "Parson's Tale" in *Works,* ed. Robinson. Caxton's unappreciative editing of the Malory MS's highly alliterative Roman Wars section speaks for itself, assuming it was Caxton and not Malory himself who edited it.

9. See Griffith "Authorship"; Hilton Kelliher, "The Early History of the Manuscript," in *Aspects of Malory,* ed. Takimiya and Brewer, 153–56.

10. Lotte Hellinga, *Caxton in Focus* (London: British Library Publications, 1984).

11. Ibid., James Spisak, introduction to *Caxton's Malory,* ed. Spisak and William Matthews (Berkeley and Los Angeles: University of California Press, 1983).

12. Roberta Florence Brinkley, *Arthurian Legend in the Seventeenth Century* (1932; reprint ed., New York: Octagon Books, 1967). Oswald and Emmeline appear in Dryden's libretto for Purcell's opera *King Arthur* of 1691 (see Chapter Four below).

13. William Caxton, epilogue to his translation of Ramon Lull, *The Boke of the Ordre of Chyualry,* ed. A. T. P. Byles, EETS o.s. 168 (London: Oxford University Press, 1926), 122.

14. Matthews, *Ill-Framed Knight,* 141–47. See also Griffith, "Authorship."

15. See Vinaver's specific comments in his editions of Malory; also Terence McCarthy, "Malory and the Alliterative Tradition," in *Studies in Malory,* ed. James W. Spisak (Kalamazoo, Mich.: Medieval Institute Publications, 1985), 53–86.

16. For complementary overviews of Malory's use of his sources, with further bibliography, see Vinaver's detailed commentary in Malory, *Works,* 3 vols, 2d ed. (Oxford: Oxford University Press, 1967); Reiss, *Malory;* James Spisak, "Introduction: Recent Trends in Malory Studies," in *Studies in Malory,* ed. Spisak, 3–4.

17. For instance, Matthews, *Ill-Framed Knight,* 141.

18. Vinaver (1978), 776; n., 699; Matthews, *Ill-Framed Knight,* 147–50 suggests that his Sir Thomas Malory might have been a prisoner of Jacques d'Armagnac in this vicinity and used his library of Arthurian works.

19. Vinaver (1978), 743; n., 135.

20. Ibid., 708; n., 777.

21. The long and tiring dispute over the "unity" of the *Morte Darthur* involving Vinaver, R. M. Lumiansky, and many others, is reviewed briefly in Spisak's introduction to *Studies in Malory,* ed. Spisak, 3. For critical material from both sides of this issue, see Vinaver's introduction to his three-volume edition; J. A. W. Bennett, ed., *Essays on Malory* (Oxford: Oxford University Press, 1963); R. M. Lumiansky, ed., *Malory's Originality* (Baltimore: Johns Hopkins University Press, 1964).

22. For example, George Saintsbury, *The English Novel* (London: J. M. Dent; New York: E. P. Dutton, 1913), 25; but there are others.

23. Alice D. Greenwood, "English Prose in the Fifteenth Century," in the *Cambridge History of English Literature,* ed. A. W. Ward and A. R. Waller (Cambridge: Cambridge University Press, 1908), 337.

24. Vinaver, introduction to his three-volume edition; see also his essay on Malory in *Arthurian Literature,* ed. Loomis, 543–46.

25. On Malory's method of breaking *entrelacement,* see Vinaver, "Sir Thomas Malory," in *Arthurian Literature,* ed. Loomis, 545–46; see also Benson, *Malory's "Morte Darthur."* Benson also outlines the three-part organization of the *Morte Darthur* described in the following pages of this chapter. Compare Bogdanow's analysis of the three-part structure of the *Suite du Merlin* in *Arthurian Literature,* ed. Loomis, 330.

26. Vinaver (1978), 730, mentions this too. Compare the prominence of Merlin in the modern works of T. H. White, Susan Cooper, Mary Stewart's

Crystal Cave series, and the related figure of Gandalf in J. R. R. Tolkien's *Lord of the Rings.*

27. For a brief account of the two Guineveres, see Jean Frappier, "The Vulgate Cycle," in *Arthurian Literature,* ed. Loomis, 299. Spenser's duplication of his heroine Una in the *Faerie Queene* revives the motif, possibly transmitted by way of Ariosto.

28. Dante Alighieri, *La divina commedia,* ed. C. H. Grandgent, revised by Charles S. Singleton (1933; reprint ed., Cambridge, Mass.: Harvard University Press, 1972), *Inferno,* canto 5, 1. 137. On Malory's presentation of the affair between Lancelot and Guinevere, see Stephen C. B. Atkinson, "Malory's Lancelot and the Quest of the Grail," in *Studies in Malory,* ed. Spisak, 129–52; and see the commentary on Malory's alteration of his sources in Vinaver's three-volume edition.

29. For *Le Bel inconnu,* see Alexandre Micha, "Miscellaneous French Romances in Verse," in *Arthurian Literature,* ed. Loomis, 370–72. Larry D. Benson's *Malory's Morte Darthur* also discusses Gareth and the "fair unknown" motif. The tale of La Cote Male Tayle occurs as book 3 of "Tristram" in Malory. See also Spisak's introduction to *Studies in Malory,* ed. Spisak, 8–9, for further comments and bibliography. Regarding the discussion of "Sir Urry" in the following paragraphs, interested readers should also see the excellent discussion in John Michael Walsh, "Malory's 'Very Mater of La Chevaler du Charyot': Characterization and Structure," in *Studies, in Malory,* ed. Spisak, 199–226.

30. A good brief description of *entrelacement* as it operates in Malory's sources may be found in Frappier, "Vulgate Cycle," 298–99. Malory's methods of rearrangement have been much discussed; two standard sources for this topic are Vinaver's comments and introductions to his editions, and Benson, *Malory's "Morte Darthur."*

31. Benson, *Malory's Morte Darthur;* Spisak, introduction to *Studies in Malory,* ed. Spisak, 7.

32. See Chapter One for discussion and bibliography on Geoffrey of Monmouth.

33. For example, Frappier, "Vulgate Cycle," 315–17.

34. For examples of fifteenth-century heraldic records, see Cartellieri, *Court of Burgundy* 124–34, 157–61. On Malory's limited use of description, see the discussions in Mark Lambert, *Malory: Style and Vision in "Le Morte Darthur"* (New Haven: Yale University Press, 1975).

35. As Vinaver says in his introduction to the one-volume edition, ix, Lambert also has much useful discussion of Malory's dialogue.

36. Benson helpfully analyzes the last books of the *Morte Darthur* in *Malory's "Morte Darthur."*

37. See Chapters One and Two on violence in Geoffrey of Monmouth, Layamon, the Alliterative *Morte Arthure,* and other works based on the

chronicle tradition; Chrétien's treatment of Arthur's character as a husband in *Le Chevalier de la charrette (The Knight of the Cart)* is considered in Chapter Two.

38. For Kei's appearance in *Culhwch,* see Chapter One. A good discussion of Kei's character in this work may be found in Richard M. Loomis's introduction to *Culhwch and Olwen,* in *Romance of Arthur,* ed. Wilhelm and Gross, 29. The early epic behavior of Kay is shown in Malory in book 4; his later degradation can be seen in the stories of Gareth, La Cote Male Tayle, and in the book of Lancelot. Steinbeck's Kay explains that his personality has been warped by bureaucratic service as Arthur's seneschal. For more discussion of Steinbeck, see Chapter Five.

39. B. J. Whiting, "Gawain, His Reputation, His Courtesy, and His Appearance in Chaucer's "Squire's Tale," *Medieval Studies* 9 (1947):189–254.

40. On this aspect of Gawain's character, see Vinaver (1978), 704.

41. Concerning the degradation of Gawain in the thirteenth-century French romances, see Chapter Two above.

42. Vinaver (1978), 66–67, 75; Gawain misbehaves notably in the episode of Pelleas and Ettarre (idem, 98–103); observe also the caution of Elaine of Astolat's father in preventing his inexperienced daughter from conducting the notorious Gawain up to her private chamber (idem, 630–31).

43. Ibid., 684 ff.

44. Romances distinguished for their interest in volatile emotional display might include the earlier French version of the non-Arthurian romance *Fleur et Blanchefleur* and the later *Claris et Laris.* In Middle English literature a variety of works suggest that particular members of the late medieval audience demanded emotional intensity in their romances, for instance *The Squire of Low Degree* and Chaucer's "Man of Law's Tale."

45. Vinaver (1978), 487.

46. For a welcome change, see Walsh, "Malory's 'Very Mater,' " who analyzes Guinevere's character with great perspicacity.

47. For example, Geoffrey of Monmouth, *History,* bk. 8, chap. 19.

48. Vinaver (1978), 81–93. On Morgan, see also Laura H. Loomis, "Gawain and the Green Knight," in *Arthurian Literature,* ed. Loomis, 535.

49. Roger Ascham, *The Scholemaster,* in *Whole Works,* ed. J. A. Giles (1864; reprint ed., New York: AMS Press, 1970), bk. 1, 159. Details of Malory's reprinting and editorial treatment in the nineteenth century as discussed in Mark Girouard, *The Return to Camelot: Chivalry and the English Gentleman* (New Haven: Yale University Press, 1981); see also Chapter Four.

50. On Sir Brunes sanz Pitie see, for instance, Vinaver (1978), 253, 417–19.

51. Compare Dinadan in Eugène Vinaver, "The Prose *Tristan,"* in *Arthurian Literature,* ed. Loomis, 344, and in Vinaver's comments on him in his three-volume edition of Malory.

52. For recent discussions of Malory's treatment of the quest of the Holy Grail that update Vinaver's commentary, see Sandra Ness Ihle, *Malory's Grail Quest* (Madison: University of Wisconsin Press, 1983) and the two important new articles by Dhira B. Mahoney and Stephen C. B. Atkinson in *Studies in Malory,* ed. Spisak. 53. Vinaver (1978), 708; n. 777.

54. Sir Philip Sidney, *An Apologie for Poetrie,* in *Elizabethan Critical Essays,* ed. G. Gregory Smith, 2 vols. (London: Oxford University Press, 1904), 1:188.

55. William Caxton, epilogue to Ramon Lull, *The Boke of the Ordre of Chyualry,* ed. A. T. P. Byles, EETS o.s. 168 (London: Oxford University Press, 1926) 122.

Chapter Four

1. John Taylor, *The Universal Chronicle of Ranulf Higden* (Oxford: Clarendon Press, 1966); Olivier de la Marche defends Arthur in his *Mémoires,* ed. Michaud and Poujoulat (Paris: 1837), 335; *Le Triumphe des neuf preux* (Abbeville, France: Pierre Gerard, 1487) has its doubts.

2. Denys Hay, *Polydore Vergil: Renaissance Historian and Man of Letters* (Oxford: Clarendon Press, 1952); Sydney Anglo, *Spectacle, Pageantry, and Early Tudor Policy* (London: Oxford University Press, 1969).

3. Both in Christopher Middleton, *The Famous Historie of Chinon of England,* ed. W. E. Mead, EETS o.s. 165 (London: Oxford University Press, 1925); see also James P. Carley, "Polydore Vergil and John Leland on King Arthur: The Battle of the Books," *Interpretations* 15 (1984):86–100.

4. Chambers, *Arthur.*

5. Roberta Florence Brinkley, *Arthurian Legends in the Seventeenth Century* (1932; reprint ed., New York: Octagon Books, 1967), 134–38.

6. Ibid.

7. Ibid.

8. Charles Bowie Millican, *Spenser and the Table Round* (Cambridge, Mass.: Harvard University Press, 1932).

9. Brinkley, *Arthurian Legends.* See also Harry M. Solomon, *Sir Richard Blackmore* (Boston: Twayne, 1980).

10. Brinkley, *Arthurian Legends;* Richard Johnson, *Tom a Lincolne,* in *A Collection of Early Prose Romances,* ed. William J. Thomas, 3 vols. (London: Pickering, 1858), 2:219–36; Middleton, *Chinon of England,* xxxii; Ascham, *Scholemaster,* bk. 1, 159.

11. William Shakespeare, *Love's Labour's Lost,* act 5, sc. 1, lines 117–54; act 5, sc. 2, lines 485–725. See Horst Schroeder, *Der topos der nine worthies in literatur und bildener kunst* (Göttingen, Germany: Vandenhoeck & Ruprecht, 1971), 128–39.

12. Brinkley, *Arthurian Legends;* Mean, Introduction to *Chinon of England* by Middleton.

13. Thomas Hughes, *The Misfortunes of Arthur,* ed. H. G. Grumbone (Berlin: Felber, 1900).

14. Ben Jonson, "The Speeches at Prince Henry's Barriers," in *Works,* ed. C. H. Herford and Percy and Evelyn Simpson, vol. 7 (1941; reprint ed. Oxford: Clarendon Press, 1963), 323–36.

15. Reproduced in Stephen Orgel and Roy Strong, *Inigo Jones: The Theatre of the Stuart Court,* 2 vols. (Berkeley and Los Angeles: University of California Press, 1973).

16. Mark Dominik, *William Shakespeare and the Birth of Merlin* (New York: Philosophical Library, 1985); William Rowley, *The Birth of Merlin, or The Childe Hath Found His Father* (London: Thomas Johnson for Francis Kirkman and Henry Marsh, 1662; facsimile rpt., Amersham, Eng.: John S. Farmer, 1913).

17. John Dryden, *King Arthur,* in *The Dramatic Works,* ed. Montague Summers (1932; reprint ed., New York: Gordian Press, 1968), 231–89.

18. Brinkley, *Arthurian Legends.*

19. Alice Chandler, *A Dream of Order: The Medieval Ideal in Nineteenth-Century English Literature* (1970; reprint ed., Lincoln: University of Nebraska Press, 1971).

20. Girouard, *Return to Camelot.*

21. William Wordsworth, "The Egyptian Maid," in *Poetical Works,* ed. E. de Selincourt, 5 vols. (Oxford: Clarendon Press, 1940–49).

22. Sir Walter Scott, "The Bridal of Triermain," in *Poetical Works* (London: Longman, 1813); Christopher N. Smith, in *Arthurian Encyclopedia,* 495.

23. John Hookham Frere, *The Monks and the Giants,* ed. R. D. Waller (Manchester: Manchester University Press, 1926).

24. Thomas Love Peacock, *The Misfortunes of Elphin* (London: Hookham, 1829); Felix Felton, *Thomas Love Peacock* (London: Allen & Unwin, 1973).

25. Hallam, Lord Tennyson, introduction to Alfred, Lord Tennyson, *Idylls of the King.* Quoted in Christopher Ricks, ed., *The Poems of Tennyson* (London and New York: Longmans & W. W. Norton, 1969, 1972), 1464.

26. Hallam, Lord Tennyson, *Alfred, Lord Tennyson: A Memoir,* 2 vols. (New York: Macmillan, 1897).

27. Ricks, ed., *Poems of Tennyson,* 354–61; 1412–17; 582–98; 502–4; 610–13. See Jerome Hamilton Buckley, *Tennyson, The Growth of a Poet* (1960; reprint ed., Cambridge, Mass.: Harvard University Press, 1974), 49–50.

28. William Morris, *Collected Works,* ed. May Morris, vol. 1, *The Defense of Guenevere and Other Poems* (London: Longmans Green & Co., 1910).

29. Edgar F. Shannon, Jr., *Tennyson and the Reviewers: A Study of His Literary Reputation and the Influence of the Critics upon His Poetry, 1827–51*

(Cambridge: Mass.: Harvard University Press, 1952), 91, 95; Ricks, ed., *Poems of Tennyson,* 585; 1460; 1464.

30. Ricks, ed., *Poems of Tennyson,* 1462–65; Kathleen Tillotson, "Tennyson's Serial Poem," *Mid-Victorian Studies* (1965): 80–109.

31. Ricks, ed., *Poems of Tennyson,* 1463–65.

32. Tillotson, "Tennyson's"; Buckley, *Tennyson,* 176–91; Ricks, ed., *Poems of Tennyson,* 1463. See also John D. Rosenberg, *The Fall of Camelot: A Study of Tennyson's "Idylls of the King"* (Cambridge, Mass.: Belknap, 1973).

33. See Arthur's speech in "Guinevere" and Tennyson's epilogue; see also Buckley, *Tennyson,* 175–76.

34. See also David Staines, *Tennyson's Camelot: The "Idylls of the King" and its Medieval Sources* (Waterloo, Ontario, Canada: Wilfrid Laurier University Press, 1983).

35. Ibid.; Ricks, ed., *Poems of Tennyson,* 1525–26.

36. Staines, *Tennyson's Camelot;* Buckley, *Tennyson,* 186, 192, suggests some satire of Anglo-Catholicism may be intended in the portrayal of King Pellam.

37. Ricks, ed., *Poems of Tennyson,* 1525–26.

38. See Chapters Two and Three above; Hallam, Lord Tennyson, quoted in ibid., 1593.

39. Elaine is noticeable in the illustrations of Tennyson by W. Holman Hunt and Dante Gabriel Rossetti for the Moxon Tennyson volume. See George Somes Layard, *Tennyson and His Pre-Raphaelite Illustrators: A Book about A Book* (London: Paternoster Row, 1894). L. M. Montgomery's young Canadian heroine, Anne Shirley, takes the role of Elaine of Astolat in a reenactment of Tennyson's idyll in *Anne of Green Gables* (1908; reprint ed., New York: Grosset and Dunlap, 1970), 214–21.

40. George Bernard Shaw, review of Comyns Carr's *King Arthur, Saturday Review,* 13 January 1895. Quoted in St. John Ervine, *Bernard Shaw: His Life, Work, and Friends* (New York: William Morrow, 1956), 272.

41. See Chapter Five below, especially the discussions of Edwin Arlington Robinson and the film *Excalibur.*

42. Edward George Earle Lytton Bulwer-Lytton, *King Arthur* (London: Colburn, 1848).

43. Matthew Arnold, "Tristan and Iseult" in *Poems,* ed. Kenneth Allott, 2d ed., ed. Miriam Allott (1965; reprint ed., London and New York: Longman, 1979), 206–37.

44. Ibid., editorial notes.

45. John Christian, *Oxford Union Murals* (Chicago: University of Chicago Press, 1981).

46. Philip Henderson, *William Morris: His Life, Work, and Friends* (London: Thames & Hudson, 1967); Carole Silver, *The Romance of William Morris* (Athens: Ohio University Press, 1982).

47. Mary Morris, introduction to *Collected Works* by Morris, xix; Meredith B. Raymond, "The Arthurian Group in *The Defense of Guenevere and Other Poems,*" *Victorian Poetry* 4 (1966):213–18.

48. Georgiana Burne-Jones, *Memorials of Edward Burne-Jones,* 2 vols. (London: Macmillan, 1906); Penelope Fitzgerald, *Edward Burne-Jones, A Biography* (London: Michael Joseph, 1975); Virginia Surtees, *The Paintings and Drawings of Dante Gabriel Rossetti (1828 to 1882): A Catalogue Raisonné,* 2 vols. (Oxford: Clarendon Press, 1971); H. C. Marillier, *History of the Merton Abbey Tapestry Works* (London: Constable, 1927). See also nn. 39, 45, 46 above.

49. Lucy Bennett, *Richard Wagner: Parsifal* (Cambridge: Cambridge University Press, 1981); Stoddard Martin, *Wagner to the Waste Land: A Study of the Relationship of Wagner to English Literature* (Totowa, N.J.: Barnes & Noble, 1982); Ernest Newman, *The Wagner Operas* (New York: Knopf, 1949).

50. Algernon Charles Swinburne, *Tristram of Lyonesse* (London: Chatto & Windus, 1882); *The Tale of Balen* (London: Chatto & Windus, 1896); David Staines, "Swinburne's Arthurian World," *Studia Neophilologica* 50 (1978):53–70.

51. Sir Thomas Malory, Morte d'Arthur, 2 vols. (London: Dent, 1893–94); facsimile reproduction, *The Dent "Morte d'Arthur"* (Woodbridge, Suffolk, England: Boydell & Brewer, 1985).

52. Mark Twain, *A Connecticut Yankee in King Arthur's Court* (1889; reprint ed., New York: Webster, 1896). James Russell Lowell's "Vision of Sir Launfal" had described a knight's dream of a quest for the Holy Grail. Elisabeth Brewer and Beverley Taylor describe a good deal of nineteenth-century Arthurian literature, in particular the Southern cult of chivalry at the time of the Civil War, in *The Return of King Arthur: British and American Arthurian Literature since 1800* (Cambridge: D. S. Brewer, 1983). Sidney Lanier's adaptation of Malory in *The Boy's King Arthur* (1880) was especially influential as childhood reading.

53. J. Comyns Carr, *King Arthur: A Drama in Four Acts* (London: Macmillan, 1895)l A brief discussion appears in Brewer and Taylor, *Return of King Arthur;* see also Jennifer R. Goodman, "The Last of Avalon: Henry Irving's *King Arthur* of 1895," *Harvard Library Bulletin* 32 (1984):239–55.

Chapter Five

1. Nathan Comfort Starr, *King Arthur Today* (Gainesville: University of Florida Press, 1984); Brewer and Taylor, *Return of King Arthur;* Raymond H. Thompson, *The Return from Avalon: A Study of the Arthurian Legend in*

Modern Fiction, Contributions to the Study of Science Fiction and Fantasy, no. 14 (Westport, Conn.: Greenwood Press, 1985).

2. Edwin Arlington Robinson, *Merlin* (New York: Macmillan, 1917); *Lancelot: A Poem* (New York: Seltzer, 1920); *Tristram* (New York: Macmillan, 1927).

3. Amelia A. Rutledge on Robinson, *Arthurian Encyclopedia,* 460.

4. James Branch Cabell, *Jurgen: A Comedy of Justice* (New York: McBride, 1919).

5. T. S. Eliot, *Poems: 1909–1925* (London: Faber & Gwyer, 1925), 63–92; T. S. Eliot, *The Waste Land: A Facsimile and Transcription of the Original Drafts,* ed. Valerie Eliot (New York: Harcourt, Brace, Jovanovich, 1974), shows the editing process, with the contribution of Ezra Pound.

6. Thomas Hardy, *The Famous Tragedy of the Queen of Cornwall at Tintagel in Lyonnesse* (London and New York: Macmillan, 1923). Reviewed (with photographs) by H. W. Massingham in *T. P.'s & Cassell's Weekly,* 22 December 1923, 336; and by Ernest Brennecke, Jr., in *New York Times Magazine,* 30 December 1923.

7. John Masefield, *Badon Parchments* (London: Heinemann, 1947); *Midsummer Night and Other Tales in Verse* (London: Heinemann, 1928); *Tristan and Isolt: A Play in Verse* (London: Heinemann; New York: Macmillan, 1927); *Basilissa* (London: Heinemann, 1940). Brewer and Taylor, *Return of King Arthur,* discuss Masefield, 225–32.

8. John Masefield, *The Midnight Folk* (London: Heinemann, 1927); *The Box of Delights* (London: Heinemann, 1935).

9. Sylvia Townsend Warner, *T. H. White: A Biography* (New York: Viking Press, 1967), foreword and 55 ff.

10. Brewer and Taylor, *Return of King Arthur,* 261; Charles Williams, *Taliessin through Logres* (Oxford: Oxford University Press, 1938); *The Region of the Summer Stars* (London: Oxford University Press, 1944); *The Figure of Arthur,* in Charles Williams and C. S. Lewis, *Arthurian Torso* (London: Oxford University Press, 1948). On the Oxford Inklings group, see Charles Moorman, *The Precincts of Felicity: The Augustinian City of the Oxford Christians* (Gainesville: University of Florida Press, 1966). For interpretations of Williams's poetry, see Brewer and Taylor, *Return of King Arthur,* 245–61; C. S. Lewis, *Williams and The Arthuriad* in *Arthurian Torso;* Glen Cavaliero, *Charles Williams: Poet of Theology* (London: Macmillan, 1983); Karl Heinz Göller, "From Logres to Carbonek: The Arthuriad of Charles Williams," *Arthurian Literature* 1 (1981):121–73.

11. Brewer and Taylor *Return of King Arthur;* Lewis, *Williams and the Arthuriad.*

12. Brewer and Taylor, *Return of King Arthur,* 256–58, especially "Taliesin in the Rose Garden" and "The Departure of Dindrane."

13. Charles Williams, *The War in Heaven* (London: Victor Gollancz, 1930); Brewer and Taylor, *Return of King Arthur,* 242–45.

14. C. S. Lewis, *That Hideous Strength: A Modern Fairy Tale for Grownups* (London: Lane, 1945); Paul Holmer, *C. S. Lewis: The Shape of His Faith and Thought* (New York: Harper & Row, 1976).

15. Tolkien and Gordon, eds., *Sir Gawain and the Green Knight;* J. R. R. Tolkien, trans., *Sir Gawain and the Green Knight, Pearl, and Sir Orfeo* (London: Allen & Unwin, 1975). The final volume of Tolkien's *Lord of the Rings* trilogy appeared in 1956.

16. John Cowper Powys, *A Glastonbury Romance* (New York: Simon & Schuster, 1932); *Porius, A Romance of the Dark Ages* (London: Macdonald, 1951); *Morwyn, or the Vengeance of God* (London: Cassell, 1937) is less directly Arthurian—Merlin and Taliesin appear briefly in the course of the main characters' journey.

17. John Steinbeck, preface to *Tortilla Flat* (1935).

18. James Joyce, *Finnegans Wake* (London: Faber & Faber, 1939).

19. T. H. White, *The Once and Future King* (London: Collins, 1958); Warner, *T. H. White.*

20. Warner, *T. H. White,* 38, 98.

21. Ibid., 129–30.

22. Ibid., 148–49.

23. T. H. White, *The Book of Merlyn,* ed. Sylvia Townsend Warner (Austin: University of Texas Press, 1977); Warner, *T. H. White,* 186–90.

24. Warner, preface to *The Book of Merlyn* by White, xx.

25. Alan Jay Lerner, *Camelot: Book and Lyrics* (London: Chappell, 1960).

26. Walt Disney, *The Sword in the Stone* (animated film, directed by Wolfgang Reitherman, 1963). The history of Arthurian films from Hollywood up to 1963 includes several versions of Twain's *Connecticut Yankee* including a 1931 film with Will Rogers and Maureen O'Sullivan, and the 1949 Bing Crosby vehicle. The 1953 spectacular *Knights of the Round Table* starring Robert Taylor and Ava Gardner, was perhaps a more representative effort.

27. Vladimir Nabokov, "Lance," in *Nabokov's Dozen* (New York: Doubleday, 1958); Ezra Pound, *Cantos,* no. xci (1955); Thomas Gunn, "Merlin in the Cave: He Speculates without a Book," in *The Sense of Movement* (1957; rpt. Chicago: University of Chicago Press, 1959), 56–58; Geoffrey Hill, "Merlin," in *For the Unfallen* (London: 1959); other more ambitious poems on Arthurian subjects include Martin Skinner's *Merlin, or The Return of Arthur, A Satiric Epic* (1951) and *The Return of Arthur: A Poem of the Future* (1955), and John Heath-Stubbs, *Artorius* (1973).

28. Bernard Malamud, *The Natural* (New York: Harcourt, Brace & Co., 1952). Like Robinson's *Tristram, The Natural* won a Pulitzer prize.

29. Henry Treece, *The Eagles Have Flown* (London: Allen & Unwin, 1954); *The Great Captains* (London: Bodley Head, 1956; *The Green Man*

(New York: Putnam, 1966); see Margery Fisher, *Henry Treece* (London: Bodley Head, 1969).

30. Rosemary Sutcliff, *The Lantern Bearers* (London: Oxford University Press, 1959); Thompson, *Return from Avalon.*

31. Naomi Mitchinson, *To the Chapel Perilous* (London: Allen & Unwin, 1955); see Thompson, *Return from Avalon;* Marion K. Nellis, "Anachronistic Humor in Two Arthurian Romances of Education: *To the Chapel Perilous* and *The Sword and the Stone,*" *Studies in Medievalism* 2 (1983):57–78.

32. Rosemary Sutcliff, *Sword at Sunset* (London: Hodder & Stoughton, 1963). Sutcliff's more recent works recount the legends for juvenile readers: *The Light beyond the Forest: The Quest for the Holy Grail* (London: Bodley Head, 1979); *The Road to Camlann* (London: Bodley Head, 1981); *The Sword and the Circle: King Arthur and the Knights of the Round Table* (London: Bodley Head, 1981); *Tristan and Iseult* (London: Bodley Head, 1971).

33. Arthur Quiller-Couch and Daphne du Maurier, *Castle Dor* (London: Dent, 1961).

34. Alan Garner, *The Wierdstone of Brisingamen: A Tale of Alderley,* rev. ed. (Harmondsworth, England: Penguin, 1963); *The Moon of Gomrath* (London: Collins, 1963).

35. André Norton, *Witch World* (New York: Ace, 1963); *Steel Magic* (Cleveland: World, 1965; republished as *Grey Magic,* 1967). See Thompson, *Return from Avalon.*

36. André Norton, *Merlin's Mirror* (New York: DAW, 1975).

37. Mary Stewart, *The Crystal Cave* (London: Hodder & Stoughton; New York: William Morrow, 1970); *The Hollow Hills* (London: Hodder & Stoughton; New York: William Morrow, 1973); *The Last Enchantment* (London: Hodder & Stoughton; New York: William Morrow, 1979).

38. Mary Stewart, *The Wicked Day* (London: Hodder & Stoughton; New York: William Morrow, 1983); reviewed, Virginia M. S. Kennedy, *Studies in Medievalism,* 2 (1983):117–19.

39. John Steinbeck, *The Act of King Arthur and His Noble Knights,* ed. Chase Horton (New York: Farrar, Straus, & Giroux, 1976).

40. Brewer and Taylor, *Return of King Arthur,* 298.

41. Walker Percy, *Lancelot* (New York: Farrar, Straus, & Giroux, 1978).

42. Thomas Berger, *Arthur Rex: A Legendary Novel* (New York: Delacorte, 1978). Brewer and Taylor, *Return of King Arthur,* 298–300.

43. Susan Cooper, *Over Sea, under Stone* (New York: Harcourt, Brace and World; London: Cape, 1965); *The Dark Is Rising* (New York: Athenaeum, 1973); *Greenwitch* (New York: Athenaeum, 1974); *The Grey King* (New York: Athenaeum, 1975); *Silver on the Tree* (New York: Athenaeum, 1977).

44. Victor Canning, *The Crimson Chalice* (New York: Morrow, 1978).

45. Richard Monaco, *Parsival, or a Knight's Tale* (New York: Macmillan; London: MacDonald and James, 1977); *The Grail War* (New York: Pocket Books, 1979); *The Final Quest* (New York: Putnam, 1980).

46. Robert Nye, *Merlin* (New York: Putnam, 1979).

47. Alice Grellner, Raymond H. Thompson, *Arthurian Encyclopedia,* 181–83.

48. Parke Godwin, *Firelord* (New York: Doubleday, 1980); *Beloved Exile* (New York: Bantam, 1984); *The Last Rainbow* (New York: Bantam, 1985).

49. Gillian Bradshaw, *Hawk of May* (New York: Simon & Schuster, 1980); *Kingdom of Summer* (New York: Simon & Schuster, 1981); *In Winter's Shadow* (New York: Simon & Schuster, 1982); Sharan Newman, *Guinevere* (New York: St. Martin's, 1981); *The Chessboard Queen* (New York: St. Martin's 1984); *Guinevere Evermore* (New York: St. Martin's, 1985); reviewed by Mildred Leake Day in *Studies of Medievalism* 2 (1983):111–12.

50. Screenplay by John Boorman and Rospo Pallenberg; Norris J. Lacy, *Arthurian Encyclopedia,* 57.

51. C. J. Cherryh, *Port Eternity* (New York: DAW, 1982).

52. Roderick MacLeish, *Prince Ombra* (New York: Tom Doherty Associates, 1982).

53. Phillis Ann Karr, *Idylls of the Queen* (New York: Ace, 1982).

54. Mike W. Barr and Brian Bolland, *Camelot 3000* (New York: DC Comics, 1980–84); reviewed by Sally K. Slocum, *Studies in Medievalism* 2 (1983):113–16.

55. Marion Zimmer Bradley, *The Mists of Avalon* (New York: Knopf, 1982); reviewed by Freya Reeves Lambides, *Studies in Medievalism* 2 (1983):107–10.

56. Richard Monaco, *Runes* (New York: Ace, 1984); *Broken Stone* (New York: Ace, 1985).

57. David Lodge, *Small World* (1984: rpt. New York: Warner, 1986).

Selected Bibliography

PRIMARY SOURCES

1. Historical Works

Bede, *Opera Historica.* Edited by Charles Plummer. London: Clarendon Press, 1896.

Geoffrey of Monmouth. *Historia regum Britanniae.* Edited by Acton Griscom. London: Longmans Green & Co., 1929.

Gerald of Wales. *Giraldi Cambrensis opera.* Edited by J. S. Brewer, J. F. Dimock, and G. F. Warner. Rolls Series. 8 vols. London: Longman, 1861–92.

Gildas. *De excidio Brittanniae.* Edited and translated by Michael Winterbottom, as *The Ruin of Britain.* In *History from the Sources,* vol. 7. Chichester, England: Phillimore, 1978.

Leland, John. *Assertio inclytissimi Arturii.* Edited by William Edward Mead. In Christopher Middleton, *The Famous Historie of Chinon of England,* 91–150. EETS o.s. 165. London: Oxford University Press, 1925.

Nennius. *Historia Brittonum.* Edited and translated by John Morris, as *British History and the Welsh Annals.* In *History from the Sources,* vol. 8. Chichester, England: Phillimore, 1980.

William of Malmesbury. *Gesta regum Anglorum.* In *Willelmi Malmesbiriensis monachi de gestis regum Anglorum libri quinque,* edited by William Stubbs. 2 vols. London: Eyre & Spottiswoode, 1887–89.

2. Prose and Verse Romances

Béroul. *Le Roman de Tristan.* Edited by Ernest Muret. Paris: Champion, 1962.

Chaucer, Geoffrey, *Works.* Edited by F. N. Robinson. 2d ed. Boston: Houghton Mifflin, 1957.

Chrétien de Troyes. *Les Romans de Chrétien de Troyes. Vol. 1, Erec et Enide,* edited by Mario Roques. Paris: Champion, 1970. Vol. 2, *Cligès,* edited by Alexandre Micha. Paris: Champion, 1958. Vol. 3, *Le Chevalier de la charrette,* edited by Mario Roques. Paris: Champion, 1969. Vol. 4, *Le Chevalier au lion,* edited by Mario Roques. Paris: Champion, 1970. *Le Roman de Perceval (Le Conte du Graal),* edited by William Roach. Paris and Geneva: Minard & Droz, 1959.

Day, Mildred Leake, ed. and trans. *The Rise of Gawain, Nephew of Arthur (De ortu Waluuanii nepotis Arturi)*. New York: Garland, 1984.

Gottfried von Strassburg. *Tristan*. Edited by Reinhold Bechstein. Reedited by Peter Ganz. Wiesbaden, Germany: Brockhaus, 1978.

Hissinger, P. F., ed. *Le Morte Arthure, A Critical Edition*. The Hague: Mouton, 1975.

Kennedy, Elspeth, ed. *Lancelot do Lac: The Non-cyclic Old French Prose Romance*. 2 vols. Oxford: Clarendon Press, 1980.

Krishna, Valerie, ed. *The Alliterative Morte Arthure, A Critical Edition*. New York: Franklin, 1976.

Malory, Sir Thomas. *Works*. Edited by Eugène Vinaver. 3 vols. in 1. 1971. Reprint. Oxford: Oxford University Press, 1978.

Malory, Sir Thomas. *Works*. Edited by Eugène Vinaver. 3 vols. 1947. 2d ed. Oxford: Oxford University Press, 1967.

Marie de France. *Lais*. Edited by Alfred Ewert. Oxford: Blackwell, 1960.

Micha, Alexandre, ed. *Lancelot: roman en prose du xiiie siècle*. 7 vols. Geneva: Droz, 1978–80.

Micha, Alexandre, ed. *Merlin, roman du xiiie siècle*. Geneva: Droz, 1979.

Pauphilet, Albert, ed. *La Queste del Saint Graal*. Paris: Champion, 1923.

Sands, D.B., ed. *Middle English Romances*. New York: Holt, Rinehart, & Winston, 1966.

Sommer, H. Oskar, ed. *The Vulgate Version of the Arthurian Romances*. 8 vols. Washington, D.C.: Carnegie Institution, 1908–16.

Thomas. *Les Fragments du roman de Tristan, poème du xiie siècle*, edited by B. H. Wind. Geneva: Droz, 1960.

Tolkien, J. R. R., and E. V. Gordon, eds. *Sir Gawain and the Green Knight*. 2d ed., edited by Norman Davis. Oxford: Clarendon Press, 1967.

Wace, *Le Roman de Brut*. Edited by I. Arnold. 2 vols. Paris: SATF, 1938–40.

Wace, *Le Roman de Rou*. Edited by A. J. Holden. 3 vols. Paris: SATF, 1970–73.

3. Novels

Berger, Thomas. *Arthur Rex: A Legendary Novel*. New York: Delacorte, 1978.

Bradley, Marion Zimmer. *The Mists of Avalon*. New York: Knopf, 1982.

Bradshaw, Gillian. *Hawk of May*. New York: Simon & Schuster, 1980.

Canning, Victor. *The Crimson Chalice*. New York: Morrow, 1978.

Cherryh, C. J. *Port Eternity*. New York: DAW, 1982.

Cooper, Susan. *Over Sea, under Stone*. London: Cape, 1965.

Garner, Alan. *The Wierdstone of Brisingamen. A Tale of Alderley*. 1960. Rev. ed. Harmondsworth, England: Penguin, 1963.

Godwin, Parke. *Firelord*. New York: Doubleday, 1980.

Karr, Phillis Ann. *Idylls of the Queen*. New York: Ace, 1982.

Lewis, C. S. *That Hideous Strength: A Modern Fairy Tale for Grownups.* London: Lane, 1945.

Lodge, David. *Small World.* New York: Macmillan, 1984: rpt. New York: Warner, 1986.

Malamud, Bernard. *The Natural.* New York: Harcourt, Brace & Co., 1952.

Masefield, John. *Badon Parchments.* London: Heinemann, 1947.

Monaco, Richard. *Parsival, or A Knight's Tale.* New York: Macmillan, 1977.

Newman, Sharan. *Guinevere.* New York: St. Martin's, 1981.

Peacock, Thomas Love. *The Misfortunes of Elphin.* In *Works,* edited by H. F. B. Brett-Smith and C. E. Jones, vol. 4. 1829. Reprint. New York: AMS Press, 1967.

Percy, Walker, *Lancelot.* New York: Farrar, Straus, & Giroux, 1978.

Powys, John Cowper. *A Glastonbury Romance.* New York: Simon & Schuster, 1932.

Quiller-Couch, Arthur, and Daphne du Maurier. *Castle Dor.* London: Dent, 1962.

Steinbeck, John. *The Acts of King Arthur and His Noble Knights.* Edited by Chase Horton. New York: Farrar, Straus, & Giroux, 1976.

Stewart, Mary. *The Crystal Cave.* London: Hodder & Stoughton, 1970; New York: William Morrow, 1970.

Sutcliffe, Rosemary. *Sword at Sunset.* London: Hodder & Stoughton, 1963.

Twain, Mark [Samuel Clemens]. *A Connecticut Yankee in King Arthur's Court.* 1889. Reprint. New York: Modern Library, 1917.

White, Terence Hanbury. *The Book of Merlyn.* Austin: University of Texas Press, 1977.

White, T. H. *The Once and Future King.* London: Collins, 1958; New York: G. P. Putnam's Sons, 1958.

Williams, Charles. *The War in Heaven.* London: Victor Gollancz, 1930.

4. Poems

Arnold, Matthew. "Tristram and Iseult." In *Poems,* edited by Kenneth Allott. 2d ed., edited by Miriam Allott, 206–37. 1965. Reprint. London and New York: Longman, 1979.

Bromwich, Rachel, ed. *Trioedd Ynys Prydein: The Welsh Triads.* 1961. Rev. ed. Cardiff: University of Wales Press, 1978.

Bulwer-Lytton, Edward George Earle Lytton. *King Arthur.* London: Colburn, 1848.

Eliot, T. S. *The Waste Land.* In *Poems: 1909–1925.* London: Faber & Gwyer, 1925.

Frere, John Hookham. *The Monks and the Giants.* Edited by R. D. Waller. Manchester: Manchester University Press, 1926.

Jackson, Kenneth, ed. *The Gododdin: The Oldest Scottish Poem.* Edinburgh: Edinburgh University Press, 1969.

Layamon. *Brut*. Edited by G. L. Brook and R. F. Leslie. EETS o.s. 250, 277. 2 vols. London: Oxford University Press, 1963, 1978.

Morris, William. *The Defence of Guenevere and Other Poems*. In *Collected Works*, vol. 1. Edited by May Morris. London: Longmans Green & Co., 1910.

Robinson, Edwin Arlington. *Tristram*. New York: Macmillan, 1927.

Scott, Sir Walter. "The Bridal of Triermain." In *Poetical Works*. London: Longman, 1813.

Swinburne, Algernon Charles. *Tristram of Lyonesse* and *The Tale of Balen*. In *Poems*, vol. 4: 5–151; 153–233. London: Chatto & Windus, 1905.

Tennyson, Alfred, Lord. *The Poems of Tennyson*. Edited by Christopher Ricks. London: Longmans, 1969.

Williams, Charles. *Taliessin through Logres*. 1938. Reprint. London: Oxford University Press, 1969.

Wordsworth, William. "The Egyptian Maid." In *Poetical Works*, edited by E. de Selincourt. 5 vols. Oxford: Clarendon Press, 1940–49.

5. Other Prose Works

Evans, J. Gwenogvyrn, ed. *The White Book Mabinogion*. Pwyllheli, Wales: n.p., 1907.

Rhys, Sir John, ed. *The Text of the Mabinogion and Other Welsh Tales from the Red Book of Hergest*. Oxford: J. G. Evans, 1887.

6. Plays

Dryden, John. *King Arthur*. In *The Dramatic Works*, edited by Montague Summers, 231–89. 1932. Reprint. New York: Gordian Press, 1968.

Hardy, Thomas. *The Famous Tragedy of the Queen of Cornwall at Tintagel in Lyonnesse*. London and New York: Macmillan, 1923.

Hughes, Thomas. *The Misfortunes of Arthur*. Edited by H. G. Grumbone. Berlin: Felber, 1900.

Jonson, Ben. "The Speeches at Prince Henry's Barriers." In *Works*, edited by C. H. Herford and Percy and Evelyn Simpson, 7: 323–36. 1941. Reprint. Oxford: Clarendon Press, 1963.

Lerner, Alan Jay. *Camelot: Book and Lyrics*. London: Chappell, 1960.

Masefield, John. *Tristan and Isolt: A Play in Verse*. London: Heinemann; New York: Macmillan, 1927.

Rowley, William. *The Birth of Merlin, or The Childe Hath Found His Father*. London: Thomas Johnson for Francis Kirkman and Henry Marsh, 1662. Facsimile reprint, Amersham, England: John S. Farmer, 1913.

7. Other Works

Mike W. Barr and Brian Bolland, *Camelot 3000*. 12 issues. New York: DC Comics, 1980–84.

SECONDARY SOURCES

1. Bibliographies

Bulletin bibliographique de la société internationale Arthurienne, Bibliographical Bulletin of the International Arthurian Society, vols. 1–35 (1949–83). Standard reference for works on Arthurian topics, updated annually. (Editor, Douglas Kelly).

Jost, Jean E. *Ten Middle English Arthurian Romances: A Reference Guide.* Boston: G. K. Hall, 1986.

Pickford, Cedric E., and Rex Last, eds. *The Arthurian Bibliography.* Vol. 1, *Author Listing.* Cambridge: Brewer, 1981.

Pickford, Cedric E., and Rex Last, eds. *The Arthurian Bibliography.* Vol. 2, *Subject Index.* Cambridge: Brewer, 1983.

Last, Rex, ed. *The Arthurian Bibliography.* Vol. 3. Cambridge: Brewer, 1985.

Parry, John J., ed. *Bibliography of Critical Arthurian Literature for the Years 1922–29.* New York: MLA, 1931 and continuations 1941–63 in *MLQ.*

Reiss, Edmund, Louise Horner Reiss, and Beverly Taylor. *Arthurian Legend and Literature: An Annotated Bibliography.* Vol. 1, *The Middle Ages.* New York: Garland, 1984.

Also useful for current bibliography and information on Arthurian studies are several Arthurian journals and annual volumes:

Barber, Richard, ed. *Arthurian Literature.* vols. 1–6 Cambridge, Engl: D. S. Brewer, and Totowa, N.J.: Barnes & Noble, 1981–86. Annual volume.

Day, Mildred Leake, ed. *Quondam et Futurus.* Newsletter of Arthurian Studies.

Lambides, Freya Reeves, publisher. *Avalon to Camelot.* Arthurian studies quarterly.

Peyton, Henry Hall III, ed. *Arthurian Interpretations.* Journal on Arthurian literature.

Sumberg, Lewis, ed. *Tristania.* Tristan studies journal.

2. Books

Alcock, Leslie. *Arthur's Britain: History and Archaeology* A.D. *367–634.* London: Penguin, 1971. A standard account of recent historical and archaeological work.

Ashe, Geoffrey. *The Discovery of King Arthur.* Garden City, N.Y.: Anchor, Doubleday, 1985. Reflects recent ideas about the historical Arthur.

Barber, Richard W. *Arthur of Albion.* New York: Barnes & Noble, 1961. A good general discussion of the legend and literature.

Barber, Richard. *The Figure of King Arthur.* London: Longman, 1972. A useful contrasting analysis of the historical evidence.

Benson, Larry D. *Art and Tradition in "Sir Gawain and the Green Knight."* New Brunswick, N.J.: Rutgers University Press, 1965. An essential study of this important romance.

Benson, Larry D. *Malory's "Morte Darthur."* Cambridge, Mass.: Harvard University Press, 1976. Analyzes Malory within his literary and historical context.

Brinkley, Roberta Florence. *Arthurian Legends in the Seventeenth Century.* 1932. Reprint. New York: Octagon Books, 1967. The standard work on Arthurian literature in this period.

Bruce, James Douglas. *The Evolution of Arthurian Romance from the Beginnings Down to the Year 1300.* 2d ed. 2 vols. Baltimore: Johns Hopkins University Press, 1928. Still a very useful comprehensive account of the subject.

Chambers, E. K. *Arthur of Britain.* London: Sidgwick & Jackson, 1927. A readable and sensible discussion of early Arthurian materials.

Frappier, Jean. *Chrétien de Troyes.* Paris: Hatier, 1957. A classic study of this important author.

Hay, Denys. *Polydore Vergil: Renaissance Historian and Man of Letters.* Oxford: Clarendon Press, 1952. The standard English reference on the historian and his work.

Lacy, Norris J., et al., eds. *The Arthurian Encyclopedia.* New York: Garland, 1986. A very useful reference volume.

Loomis, Roger Sherman, ed. *Arthurian Literature in the Middle Ages: A Collaborative History.* London: Oxford University Press, 1959. This is still the essential reference for medieval Arthurian works.

Loomis, Roger Sherman. *The Development of Arthurian Romance.* New York: Harper & Row, 1963. An overview of the subject by a key scholar of this century.

Loomis, Roger Sherman, ed. *Wales and the Arthurian Legend.* Cardiff: University of Wales Press, 1956. This volume investigates the Celtic role in the Arthurian legend.

Loomis, Roger Sherman, and Laura Hibbard Loomis. *Arthurian Legends in Medieval Art.* London: Oxford University Press, 1938. This is still the fundamental study in its field.

Merriman, James Douglas. *The Flower of Kings: A Study of the Arthurian Legend in England between 1485 and 1835.* Lawrence: University Press of Kansas, 1973. A useful study of this neglected period of Arthurian literature.

Moorman, Charles and Ruth. *An Arthurian Dictionary.* Jackson: University Press of Mississippi, ca. 1978. Reference for Arthurian names and other topics.

Morris, John. *The Age of Arthur.* New York: Scribner, 1973. Reassesses the historical evidence in a new way.

Rosenberg, John D. *The Fall of Camelot: A Study of Tennyson's "Idylls of the King."* Cambridge, Mass.: Belknap, 1973. An important critical study of this poem.

Staines, David. *Tennyson's Camelot: The "Idylls of the King" and Its Medieval Sources.* Waterloo, Ontario, Canada: Wilfrid Laurier University Press, 1983. The most detailed account of Tennyson's use of his sources.

Starr, Nathan Comfort. *King Arthur Today: The Arthurian Legend in English and American Literature, 1901–1953.* Gainesville: University of Florida Press, 1954. One of the key references on modern Arthurian literature.

Brewer, Elisabeth, and **Beverley Taylor.** *The Return of King Arthur: British and American Arthurian Literature since 1800.* Cambridge: D. S. Brewer, 1983. Among the most comprehensive studies of this period.

Thompson, Raymond H. *The Return from Avalon: A Study of the Arthurian Legend in Modern Fiction.* Contributions to the Study of Science Fiction and Fantasy, no. 14. Westport, Conn.: Greenwood Press, 1985. Describes a large number of modern Arthurian fictional works.

Vinaver, Eugène. *The Rise of Romance.* Oxford: Clarendon, 1971. An important account of the development of the romance.

Warner, Sylvia Townsend. *T. H. White: A Biography.* New York: Viking Press, 1967. The standard critical biography of White.

3. Articles

Ashe, Geoffrey. " 'A Certain Very Ancient Book': Traces of an Arthurian Source in Geoffrey of Monmouth's *History.*" *Speculum* 56 (1981):301–23. Here Ashe reinvestigates the historicity of Arthur in a new way.

Dumville, David. "Sub-Roman Britain: History and Legend." *History* 62 (1977):173–92.

———. "The Historical Value of the *Historia Brittonum.*" *Arthurian Literature* 6 (1986):1–26. These are both important historical reassessments.

Loomis, Laura Hibbard. "Arthur's Round Table." *PMLA* 41 (1926):771–84. One of the basic discussions of this important subject.

Index